"How to" guide

SECOND EDITION

Building a Fundraising Database Using your PC

A step by step guide for voluntary organisations

GW00697443

Peter Flory

DIRECTORY OF SOCIAL CHANGE

CAF

WHAT EACH SECTION CONTAINS

Section 1 – 'Before you start'

This section explains how a database can be of assistance during a fundraising campaign, discusses the necessary hardware and software and concludes with suggestions as to how to capture and use the data you will need.

Section 2 – 'The beginner's database'

As its title suggests, this section is for beginners in IT who have the basic experience described above under 'Who is this book for?'. Aimed at people who do not want to develop their own database, it describes how to use Microsoft Office tools together to create a database. You will learn how to:

- store information on contacts/supporters/donors (we will call them 'contacts' because fundraising databases are becoming known by the generic term 'contact databases');
- build more effective relationships;
- store details of communications with these contacts eg telephone, fax and e-mail;
- set up a fundraising campaign;
- carry out a mailing;
- record communications with contacts in non-mailing campaigns;
- record the income generated;
- analyse the income generated.

The chapters within this section give step by step instructions on how to do this, and for those who are more confident with Windows operations, a summarised version of the instructions is provided in Chapter 5. Those with more experience of databases, however, may choose to ignore this section and move straight on to Section 3.

Section 3 – 'A more advanced database'

This section is for readers who have created their own database, or have set one up using Section 2 of this book, and have experimented with different facilities. Ideally these readers will have a basic level of familiarity with Access and will have used and maintained one or more of the simple databases that are provided with every copy of Access. Section 3 shows you how to create a simple, integrated database which will enable you to do the same things as the database described in Section 2, but with the added potential to do more if you wish. As in Section 2, a summarised set of instructions is given in the final chapter of the section for the more confident user.

If you are not sure which is the right section for you, as a basic guideline, stick to Section 2 if what is covered there meets your needs, but move on to Section 3 if you are confident with Section 2, and in the future you might want to add to your database extra features that are not covered by this book.

Section 4 – 'What next?'

This gives ideas on further features you can add to your database once you have exhausted Sections 2 and/or 3, and offers guidance on where to look for help in case things go horribly wrong.

Issues you will face

Throughout the book a number of themes will recur. These include:

- whether you should have one organisational database or separate databases for separate tasks;
- how you get data out of old systems;
- what you can do on your own without any specialist assistance.

Signals you will see

Various signals are used to help you as you work through the book. These refer to hints, suggestions, warnings and notes which appear in the left-hand margin:

H = hint

S = suggestion

W = warning

N = note.

Before you start

Before you start you must know what you are trying to achieve and why you want to create a computerised database. To that end Chapter 1 will first consider how the use of a database can help you and how it fits into the traditional fundraising cycle. When you are happy that a database will be of assistance, the next task is to ensure you have suitable hardware and software available. You must then consider what data you want to store and what you want to do with it: Chapter 2 deals with this.

What do you want to achieve?

It is probably safe to assume that you want to be more effective in raising money for your particular organisation. To that end you need tools, such as databases, to help as you follow campaigns and appeals through the typical campaign cycle. A database can be defined quite simply as an accumulation of related facts. In the case of fundraising, this relates to supporters and their history of giving to a particular cause. However, this can all be recorded on cards in a filing cabinet, so why use a computer?

Why create a computerised database?

Using a computer you get speed, consistency, accuracy and the ability to handle large volumes of names, addresses, letters and income items. For example you can:

- save time by producing standard letters – by using a good quality printer and appropriate salutations they can appear as though they were individually written for each supporter;
- always address people consistently and accurately;
- ensure that supporters get what they want when they want it – for instance people may say 'only send me appeal mailings at Christmas';
- save time, resources and money by better targeting of mailings;
- thank people quickly by producing tailored thank you letters when a donation is received – here speed is of the essence because donors expect an efficient 'banking and thanking' procedure;
- be more responsive to people when they telephone by bringing up their computer record as you are speaking to them;
- maintain different records for different types of supporters – some of the information you store about grant-making trusts (eg giving policy, meeting dates etc) is quite different from the information you store about individual donors, yet there is data common to both (eg amounts given and when);
- analyse income data quickly to determine the effectiveness of a campaign;

- analyse other data about your supporters to determine who they are, where they live, what they are interested in;
- make more informed management decisions based on the information provided by your analyses;
- provide feedback on the results of fundraising campaigns to supporters, managers, trustees etc.

THE FUNDRAISING CYCLE

The following simple diagram (Figure 1) shows the major elements of most fundraising campaigns. Using this as our guide, we can see how a database can provide benefits at each stage of the cycle (Table 1).

Figure 1 The fundraising cycle

1. Making the case

2. Research

3. Strategy

4. Monitoring

One database or several?

The ideal situation is to have one single database, as described in Section 3. This avoids duplication of records as well as the possibility of duplicate mailings, and ensures that all forms of contact with every supporter are recorded in the same place no matter who in your organisation makes the contact. However, there is a price to pay for a single organisational database and that is complexity. The database needs to be complex to cater for the different needs associated with the different types of supporters. If you are not experienced in using databases, it might be easier for you to keep two or three separate ones; to do this, follow Section 2. There is no problem with this approach, particularly if every supporter appears on only one of the databases.

Table 1 How databases can help in fundraising

Fundraising tasks	How a database can help you
1 Making the case • Deciding what the appeal is • Clarifying the target sum • Breaking appeal down into manageable targets • Selling the benefits	Feeding in information from previous campaigns will help you to: • Decide whether the appeal is for general or specific purposes or both • Work out how much money you need in total • Identify specific projects that will raise the funds to meet your targets • Decide who might be interested in the projects and what they will need to know • Define what difference the appeal will make
2 Research • Who has supported you in the past? • Can you ask them again? • When do they want (or not want) to hear from you? • Contact details	Once you have input all your contact data you can make enquiries of the system, segment the database and run selections for a range of purposes to find out: • What did past supporters give – money, time or both? • How much did they give – amount? • How did they choose to give – method? • How often can you communicate with them? • What are they interested in supporting? • What specific mailings are appropriate – eg Christmas, special events? • How to get the right message to the right person at the right time
3 Strategy • Deciding on the different methods you will use to ask for support • Timetable activities and assign targets	Mail merges make it possible to target potential donors accurately and speedily. You can: • Target an individual, groups or all contacts for mailings, poster campaigns etc • Record all details of communications with contacts • Work out which methods achieve greatest success • Find out whether you got the money you thought you would • See where you should be investing resources to maximise the effect

4 Monitoring and consolidation
 	
• Communicating with donors and supporters
• Analysing response rates
• Management information
• Market research, project appraisal
• Planning realistic appeals
• Obtaining commitment from managers/trustees
• Making decisions about what resources are needed to raise funds
	Databases can help you:
	• Thank donors quickly and appropriately
	• Update your database
	• Generate financial and other activity reports, eg
	  – how much money was raised and from where?
	  – calculating cost return ratios
	  – patterns of giving
	  – average gift values
	  – where your best supporters are
	  – what do (or can) they give?
	• Feed all information back into next year's fundraising plans:
	  – what is possible based on what you know you can do?
	  – what investment might be needed next time?

The equipment

If you are now convinced of the benefits of a computer database then you will need some suitable equipment and some software to create the database.

HARDWARE YOU WILL NEED

In order to work through this book you will need a PC with at least 64Mb of RAM (memory), at least 4Gb of disk and a CD-ROM drive. All PCs come with a floppy disk drive but it is also advisable to have some sort of tape device (a 'tape streamer') or CD writer/rewriter to take a copy of (back up) your work because you will soon find that your database will not fit on a floppy disk. It is very important to back up, not just your database, but everything stored on your computer's disk because, in very rare circumstances, disks malfunction and the data stored on them is unreadable. If this happens, or the computer fails in some other way, and you have a back-up tape then you can load your data onto a new disk, or even a new computer, and continue to work. You will also need a good quality printer (laser or inkjet), but preferably a laser printer capable of printing at least eight pages per minute if you are going to do mailings from your database.

SOFTWARE YOU WILL NEED

You do not need anything complex. We have chosen Microsoft products because they are so widely used.

For Section 2 you will need Microsoft Windows 95/98/Me/2000 and any version of Microsoft Office 2000. This can be Small Business Edition, Standard, Professional or Premium, because all we will be using is Outlook, Word and Excel.

For Section 3 you will need Microsoft Windows 95/98/Me/2000 and Microsoft Office 2000 Professional or Premium because we will be using Access.

If you don't have a suitable PC at the moment and you have to buy one, then get one with the software already loaded. Although it is quite easy to load the software from a CD, it is easier still if you can unpack your PC, plug it in and begin.

Cost

It is not practical to recommend specific makes of equipment because there are so many to choose from and some suppliers come and go quite quickly. The figures given below are accurate at the time of writing for quality equipment from well-known names in the market place. However, please note that hardware prices change very rapidly and things may have changed considerably by the time you read this book. Hopefully they will still provide you with a useful guideline.

If you don't already have a computer then you can get a very good quality one with a higher specification than that given above for under £800 and it includes Microsoft Office 2000 Small Business Edition already loaded. If you want to create your own database with Access and you need Office Professional or Premium then it could cost you an additional £230. (A point to note – figures quoted for computer software and hardware usually exclude VAT, so the £800 PC referred to above will actually cost you up to £940.)

There are many types of back-up devices available. A popular one is the Zip drive. This holds 100Mb or 200Mb of data and will be enough to secure your database for quite some time, but it is much safer to get a tape drive that has the capacity to copy the entire contents of your hard disk. So if you have a 4.3Gb disk then get a tape that can hold 4.3Gb of data. A good quality, slow speed tape streamer should cost you no more than £150 (plus VAT) and £60 for three tapes.

A good quality, eight pages per minute (8ppm) laser printer will cost you from £160 to £230 (plus VAT) and a faster one with two paper trays will cost two to three times that amount. A good quality colour inkjet printer will cost you from £90 to £150, but the per page cost will be more than for a laser printer because the cost of replacement ink cartridges is higher than that of laser toner cartridges.

In summary, with a total investment of under £1,300 (plus VAT) consisting of £800 for the PC, £150 for the tape streamer, £230 for a laser printer and £100 for some tapes, odds and ends and a copy of this book, you are set to create your first database.

CHAPTER 2

Data, data and more data

A system starts with the data you feed into it. The more information you store and have access to about contacts and campaigns, the more effective you can be as a fundraiser. So the first major task is to define the data you need to store in the database.

The data you need to store

To create the kinds of databases described in Chapter 1 you need, at the very least, five types of data which relate to the stages of the fundraising cycle shown in brackets:

- Names and addresses of your contacts (research and strategy)
- Specific information about your contacts (research)
- Details of communications with your contacts (strategy)
- Income from your contacts (monitoring)
- Non-income responses from your contacts (monitoring).

NAMES AND ADDRESSES

Names and addresses are not as easy as they may seem. There are several traps waiting for the unwary and you must take care not to fall into them: your contacts' first impressions of your organisation are important and you need to get their names and addresses right.

The following describe real-life problems with names and addresses, all of which have caused problems for various organisations:

- not enough address lines so the district, town or county is missed off the address;
- blank lines on the address label;
- inappropriate use of types of data so a letter was addressed 'Dear Electrical Limited';
- inattention to detail so Sir Paul Jones was addressed 'Dear Sir Jones';
- inconsistencies in entering data, so for people living in North Yorkshire, some had 'North Yorkshire' under the county heading, some had 'N Yorkshire', some had 'N Yorks' and some had 'North Yorks'. This made it almost impossible to print a simple list of all the contacts living in North Yorkshire.

So what should you store?

- name – with separate sections ('fields') for the person's title, first name, other initials, surname and qualifications/honours;
- salutation – consider having a formal and informal version eg Dear Mr Jones and Dear Fred;
- address – with separate fields for at least three lines of address plus town, county and postcode (and country if you have overseas supporters);
- label/address name – for instances where you do not want to print the name as above in full on a label or envelope eg Mr P A Jones.

SPECIFIC INFORMATION

There is a huge range of information you might wish to store against contacts and many items are particular to your organisation. Some of the common ones are:

- type of contact (Individual, Company, Trust etc);
- mailing indicators/flags (note that you should make them all positive or all negative, ie avoid confusion such as 'No Mail = Yes' and 'Christmas Card = Yes'). Examples could be:
  - Appeal Mailings   Yes/No   – Telephone   Yes/No
  - Newsletter   Yes/No   – Annual Report   Yes/No
  - Raffle Tickets   Yes/No   – Christmas Card Yes/No;
- first contact source code (how you first heard of this contact);
- date of first contact;
- interest/support flags (one for every type of interest a contact might have, or for every type of support a contact might give to your organisation).

You might want to record different information for different types of contact. For example, meeting dates and giving policies for trusts, business area and sponsorship policy for corporates, and sex and birth date for individuals (birth date – not age which dates – is useful for such things as targeting mailings at different age groups and for legacy analysis).

COMMUNICATIONS

Here you can keep a record of who contacted the supporter, when, how and what about. You may want to record a telephone call to or from a contact, ad hoc mailing, appeal mailing, a fax or e-mail in or out, or an event invitation. In addition, this could be a place to record non-financial help offered or given, such as gifts in kind, sponsorship or guest speaking.

This record is especially useful for keeping track of on-going activities. If you are making applications to corporates or trusts, for example, you can record who you spoke to, when and what about, when you should contact them again, when the application should be submitted, what the result was and a reminder to apply again next year.

INCOME

It goes without saying that all income received should be recorded, but knowing how much has been given and by whom is seldom enough. You might also need to know the date it was received, the payment method (cash, cheque or standing order), your code for the appeal to which the donation related, your code for the fund to which the money was given and whether a receipt was issued or not.

You can then make various analyses of income generated, response rates and effectiveness. Amongst other things, this information could help you to decide how much to ask people for in the future, for example it is pointless sending a mailing to someone asking for £50 if the most they have ever given in the past is £5.

NON-INCOME RESPONSES

There will always be ad hoc pieces of information you would like to record against contacts, so it is useful to have a place for recording general, unstructured information.

How the data is stored

Computer people often talk in terms of files, records, fields, flat files, databases, objects and the like. With the advent of relational databases and spreadsheets, it has become common to talk about tables. A table is made up of rows and columns and the intersection of a particular row with a particular column is called a cell. The specific items of data stored in the columns are known as fields.

Earlier we mentioned five types of data that you need to store about contacts:

1 Names and addresses of your contacts
2 Specific information about your contacts
3 Details of communications you have with your contacts
4 Income you get from your contacts
5 Non-income responses or general notes on your contacts.

Whichever type of database you decide to create, you could create a table to store each type of data and thus help to manage your fundraising. However, on the principle that the fewer tables you create the easier they will be to manage, data types 1, 2 and 5 above can be consolidated into a single table. You then have a contact table, a communications table and an income table. Examples of these are given below:

CONTACTS TABLE

This lists names, addresses and other contact-related information. Each row represents a different contact and each column represents fields containing contact details such as Title, First Name, Last Name, Address Lines, Telephone Number, Date of First Communication, Interests, Notes and other similar data.

Figure 2 This is an example of a contact table in the form of a telephone list which is a standard feature of Microsoft Outlook

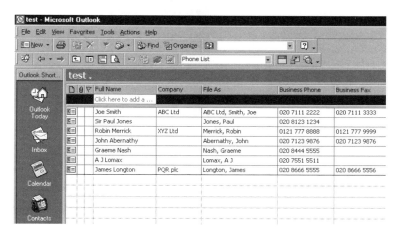

COMMUNICATIONS TABLE

This lists all the different types of communication with each contact. Each row represents a single communication with a contact and every column represents details about that communication, such as Contact Name or Number, Date, Communication Type, Result and Comments.

Figure 3 This is an example of part of a communications table in the form of a Journal list which is a standard feature of Microsoft Outlook

INCOME TABLE

This lists all the items of income you have received. Each row represents a single item of income from a single contact and every column shows the Contact Name or Number, Date, Income Amount, Appeal Code, Payment Method and anything else you wish to record.

Figure 4 This is an example of a simple income table in the form of an Excel spreadsheet

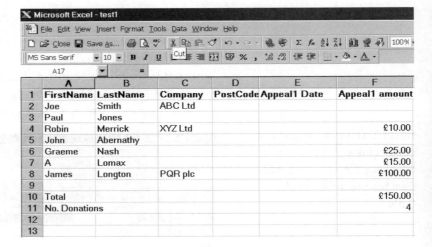

	A	B	C	D	E	F
1	FirstName	LastName	Company	PostCode	Appeal1 Date	Appeal1 amount
2	Joe	Smith	ABC Ltd			
3	Paul	Jones				
4	Robin	Merrick	XYZ Ltd			£10.00
5	John	Abernathy				
6	Graeme	Nash				£25.00
7	A	Lomax				£15.00
8	James	Longton	PQR plc			£100.00
9						
10	Total					£150.00
11	No. Donations					4
12						
13						

What to do with data from old systems

If you have contact/supporter records in paper form then you have no choice but to enter all these records manually into the computer. If you already have some records in a computer system, whether this is an obsolete database or a mail merge list of names and addresses, you may be tempted to 'convert' the records into your new database. Two simple rules of thumb may save you a lot of time and effort:

1 If there are less than 500 names and addresses then don't even think about trying to convert them. Key them in again from scratch. Even a two-fingered typist can enter 500 names and addresses in less than a week!

2 If there are considerably more than 500 names and addresses and you can get them out of the old system in a standard format, ie as a spreadsheet (Excel or Lotus) file or an ASCII, otherwise known as a CSV (comma separated values) file, then do it. You will be able to 'import' these files into your new database easily. If a standard format is not easily attainable then you will need to print out the entire database and hire a temporary data entry person to enter them all to the new database.

Importing names and addresses from old systems will be covered in Chapter 3 (page 35) and in Chapter 6 (page 96), depending on whether you are going to use Outlook or Access respectively.

How you use data

The words 'data' and 'information' are used interchangeably throughout this book but this is not strictly accurate and a distinction should be made. Data is just that, data. It has no value unless you use it and analyse it in order to draw conclusions. If you do this, you then have information.

By now you have a reasonable idea of what data items you are going to record, and Table 1 (see page 15) demonstrates how your database can be used both to store and analyse data, particularly in the research, strategy and monitoring phases of the fundraising cycle.

The Data Protection Act

A word of warning before you start using your database. You will be holding records of 'personal data'. Personal data includes names, addresses, telephone numbers, classification codes, mailing indicators, interest codes, and donation history. This means that you have to comply with the Data Protection Act.

This in turn means three things:

Note: The Information Commissioner used to be known as the Data Protection Commissioner and prior to that the Data Protection Registrar. The latest name change reflects the fact that he/she now administers the Freedom of Information Act as well as the Data Protection Act.

1   The information you hold on people (known as data subjects) and the use you make of it has to adhere to 8 principles. These principles cover things like fairness, compliance with the law, relevance, accuracy, the length of time you keep data, rights of data subjects, loss or damage, and transferring data outside of Europe.
2   A data subject can request a copy of the data you hold about him/her, the reasons you are holding it, and have the data corrected or erased where appropriate.
3   You have to 'register' with the Information Commissioner (contact details are given in Chapter 11). This is known as Notification.   **N**

Now you are ready to begin

Having thought about what data you want to record and how you are going to use that data, you are now ready to switch on the computer and start creating your first database.

The beginner's database

This section describes how to use pre-existing facilities to create a fundraising database. No 'programming' is required beyond the ability to set up a simple spreadsheet. Day to day use of the database, to assist you in the research, strategy and monitoring phases of your fundraising cycle, is also described. Chapters 3 and 4 of this section contain step by step instructions for creating and using the database, and summary instructions for the more confident users of databases are given in Chapter 5.

CHAPTER 3

Creating a simple fundraising database

This chapter describes how to set up the database. It starts by describing the tools we will use and the way in which we will use them. There is then a break point where confident users can skip to Chapter 5 (page 60) for summary instructions, or less confident users can carry on through this chapter with very detailed step by step instructions on how to set up the database.

An integrated database?

The first thing to say is that this is not an integrated database. In other words we will not be able to achieve everything we want from a single computer program, rather we will be using several programs in turn to carry out all the necessary functions. Consequently, we have to accept some limitations and compromises. Predominant amongst these will be that we are using several tools to achieve our results and we have to make them work together and keep them in step. This involves a series of tasks that must be done at each stage to maintain the integrity of the data. Forget these and you could end up with your data in a mess, but don't be put off, it is actually quite easy!

What are we going to use?

We are going to use three programs within the suite of programs known as Microsoft Office. These three programs are Outlook, Word and Excel. With these three programs we shall be able to:

- record the name, address and other details of all of our contacts;
- record communications we have with our contacts;
- select all or some of our contacts for mailing;
- produce mail-merged letters for the contacts we select;
- record donations from contacts;
- send thank you letters to donors;
- produce analysis reports on the income received.

How will Outlook, Word and Excel help us to do these things?

OUTLOOK

Outlook is a multi-purpose program which has the following sections appearing as icons down the left hand side of the screen:

- an **Inbox** section for recording details of incoming e-mails, faxes and messages;
- a **Calendar** section (a diary);
- a **Tasks** section (a 'to do' list);
- a **Journal** section (for recording communications with contacts and other actions);
- a **Notes** section (electronic post-it notes);
- a **Contacts** section.

Note: We will also be using the Journal section, but indirectly. So ignore the Journal icon on the left of the screen.

You will probably find all of these sections useful in your daily work but we will only be using the Contacts section in this book. **N** You will record everything about your contacts, except details of their gifts, within the Contacts section of Outlook.

Most of the data items you will need to create your contacts database are already defined for you in Outlook. These include:

- name (broken down into Title, First, Last and Suffix);
- three addresses (each broken down into Address Lines, Town, County and Postcode);
- four telephone numbers and three e-mail addresses;
- company name;
- job title;
- a Journal for recording your communications of all types with your contacts.

The only data items that you need to define yourself are items that are special to your organisation, such as original source code, date of first contact, your mailing flags etc. At this point you will then have to enter into Outlook the details of every contact you know to create your database (or in Outlook terms, your main folder).

WORD

Word is a traditional word processing package. Whenever you write to your contacts, whether singly or in groups, you will use Word. In the latter case you will use the mail merge facility to select all the names and addresses to be entered onto the letters automatically from Outlook. We will start by creating a mailing for everyone in your database. We will then see how you can select smaller groups of people from your database (by creating subfolders) and mail these smaller groups in the same way as the whole database.

EXCEL

Excel is a spreadsheet package which you will use to record and analyse items of income. You will copy ('export') all your contacts' names and an identifying item for each one, such as membership number or even the postcode, from Outlook into Excel. It is then the work of a few minutes to set up the spreadsheet to accept gift information and summarise it. When a gift is received from a contact you will find the contact in the Excel spreadsheet (don't worry – even if you have 2,000 contacts in your spreadsheet, it is very fast) and enter the gift details on the line for that contact. Because you set up the spreadsheet to summarise information in the first place, as you enter each gift you will be able to see immediately such things as how many gifts you have received, total income to-date and the average value of each gift.

THANK YOU LETTERS

After you have recorded the income in your database the next step is to send thank you letters to the donors. We shall look at three ways of doing this: first, by using Word on a letter-by-letter basis, second, by creating a temporary subfolder in Outlook and using it as the data source for a mail merge in Word, and third by creating a temporary Excel table to use as the data source for a mail merge in Word.

ANALYSIS AND REPORTS

At the end of your campaign you will want to analyse its effectiveness, so we will prepare a few simple reports. We already have the total campaign proceeds, the number of donations and the average donation value. As the data is stored in Excel, we can produce any number of graphs and lists from this data. Amongst the most useful ones might be your top 50 donors and a graph of number (or value) of donations over time.

ADDING NEW CONTACTS LATER

The above process works well for setting up the database and using it in the first place. Problems may arise when you add someone new to your database. Because this is not an integrated contact database system, we have to control it ourselves. We have stored details in several different places: our main folder, one or more subfolders and Excel. We will follow a set of procedures so that each is kept in step and you don't have to enter the details several times with the inherent risk of forgetting to do it or making a mistake.

Are you an experienced user of Office?

If you are an experienced user of Office and do not need step by step instructions on how to use it, then move straight to Chapter 5 (page 60) for a summary of how Office can be used to create a fundraising database. If you are not a confident Office user, and feel you need instructions at the level of which buttons to press and when, then carry on through this chapter and Chapter 4.

Setting up Outlook to record contact details

GETTING INTO OUTLOOK

In Windows there is always more than one way of doing things and some versions of the software will offer more possibilities than others. One of the following routes should get you into Outlook:

- If you have an Office Task bar on the right-hand side or the top of your screen, click the left mouse button once over the **Outlook** icon.

- If you have an **Outlook** icon on your desktop, double click on this.

- Also from your desktop, you can click **Start**, click **Programs** and then click **Microsoft Outlook**.

What you see when you open this up for the first time might be different depending on how the system was configured.

- Once Outlook is open, the important thing is to find the **Contacts** icon on the left of the screen and click that.

- If you have any dummy contacts from Microsoft, you can delete these by clicking them one at a time and then clicking **Delete** (ie the icon in the Outlook Task bar in the shape of a cross).

Figure 5 The Contacts section of Outlook will initially look like this

Note: If you don't have a Folder List icon displayed, then click the menu item **View**, then click the Toolbars item, then click the **Advanced** item. A new Toolbar will appear containing a Folder List icon.

At this stage you could rest your mouse briefly over all the other icons in the Task bar in order to familiarise yourself with what is immediately available. The most useful ones for you will be New Contact, Folder List and Find. Folder List is a 'toggle' switch, click once and it displays a list of the folders (you can think of each folder as a separate database), click again and the list disappears.

FAMILIARISING YOURSELF WITH THE STANDARD DATA FIELDS PROVIDED WITH THE SYSTEM

- Click the **New Contact** icon (not the little down arrow beside it – that gives you other options we are not interested in at the moment).
  You will see five tabs: General, Details, Activities, Certificates and All Fields.

- Click each of the tabs in turn to familiarise yourself with them and on each one, click the buttons and the drop down lists.

On the General tab you will notice a large white space in the bottom half of the screen. You can use this area to record any notes you like about the contact.

Now look particularly at the pop-up window you get when you click the Categories button (which is in the bottom left-hand corner of the screen). Judicious use of this field will help you select groups of contacts to communicate with, for instance when targeting mailings. Note that the list already contains some interesting categories like Business, Hot Contacts, Key Customer, Personal and VIP. The Master Category List button, however, allows you to delete any of the Microsoft categories and add categories of your own.

Figure 6 This is an example of what the General tab should look like after you have entered the details of your contacts

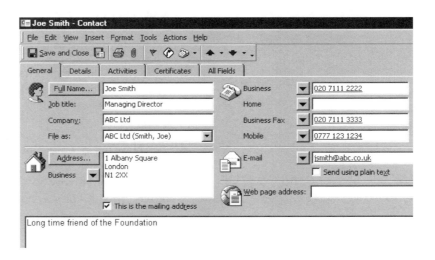

Ignore the Activities and Certificates tabs. When you get to the All Fields tab, there will be nothing to see initially. Click the drop down arrow beside the Select From field. Choose various options from the list and you can see different sets of data items in the form of a list. This is simply another way of viewing all of the fields available in the system.

You can, if you wish, design your own tab with any of the data items on it in any sequence. If you want to play with that, it is in the Tools menu. Click **Forms** and then **Design a Form** (but this should not be necessary).

CREATING YOUR OWN SPECIAL FIELDS

Recording data not in Outlook

When thinking about the research stage of your fundraising cycle, you will probably find that there are specific data items that you would like to record which are not in Outlook, such as the date of first your first communication with a contact or a note not to telephone a contact. You must decide what fields are essential for your organisation. Don't create too many. You will have to enter the data and keep them up to date. Only create the fields that you really need. You can add extra data items by the following procedures:

1 On the All Fields screen, use the scroll bar to move down the Select From list and click **User-defined Fields in Folder**. The screen will be blank.

2 Click **New**.
This gives you a pop-up window labelled New Field. The items in this window are labelled Name, Type and Format. You use this window to create any new fields you require in the system. For the purposes of this exercise, let us create three new fields: First Contact Source Code, Date of First Contact and Appeal Mailings. The first is a text field, the second is a date and the third requires a yes/no response.

3 In the Name box key in **First Contact Source Code**, leave the Type and Format boxes defaulted to Text and click **OK**. 'First Contact Source Code' appears in the previously big blank space.

4 Click **New** again, enter **Date of First Contact** in Name, click the **down arrow** against the Type box and click **Date/Time**, click the **down arrow** against the Format box, click your preferred format for displaying the date and click **OK**.

5 Click **New** again, enter **Appeal Mailings** in Name, click the **down arrow** against the Type box and click **Yes/No**, click the **down arrow** against the Format box and click **Yes/No**, then click **OK**.

You can now add any other fields that will be useful to you. You have now set up the special fields you want against your contacts and all you have to do is remember to fill them in! When you have finished creating your special fields then click on the General tab and you will be ready to record information about your contacts/supporters.

Recording and viewing information about your supporters

HOW TO ORGANISE YOUR CONTACT DATA

Before you enter your first contact, you have a decision to make – do you keep data about individuals separate from data about organisations (that is, companies, trusts, clubs and support groups) or together in the same database (or 'folder' in Outlook terms)? You need to think about this is because you will have to decide whether to file organisation records under the name of the organisation or under the name of your contact at the organisation. If you choose the former, then you have organisation names mixed up with individuals' names. If you opt for the latter, then what happens when you don't know anyone at the organisation? This is quite valid because you might make applications to grant-making trusts by simply addressing your mailings to 'The Administration Manager' or 'The Chief Executive'.

If you want to keep details of individuals and organisations separate from each other, you can do this by creating two subfolders:

1 You are currently looking at a folder called Contacts. (Make sure Contacts is highlighted.) Click **File** on the Menu bar.

2 Highlight **Folder** and click **New Folder**.

3 Fill in the **Name** (say, Individuals), leave Folder Contains defaulted to Contact Items and click **OK**.

4 You will be asked if you want a shortcut to this folder added to your Outlook Bar.
Click the box to set 'Don't prompt me about this again' and click **No**.

5 Repeat for Organisations.

You will now have two subfolders under the main Contacts folder where you can keep individuals' details and organisations' details separately.

ENTERING CONTACT DATA

For the sake of simplicity we will assume that you are going to store individuals and organisations in the same folder and file the organisations by the organisation name. To do this:

- Click the **New** icon.

- Click the **General** tab and start entering details of your first contact.

- When you have finished the first one, click the **Save And New** icon (next to the one labelled Save And Close).

Note that the system automatically creates an entry in the File As field. This field defines the order in which the records are displayed on the screen and it is used to fast search for records. For individuals (ie where you did not enter anything in the Company field) the system sets File As to Surname and First Name eg Jones, Peter.

When entering organisation records where you do not know the name of a contact, leave the Name field blank, enter the organisation name in the Company field and enter the name of the position of the person who is to receive your correspondence (eg The Chief Executive) in the Job Title field. The system will automatically fill in the File As field with the name of the organisation.

When entering organisation records where you do know the name of a contact, then put the name of the contact in the Name field, the contact's position in the Job Title field and the organisation name in the Company field. Note that the computer has automatically put the contact's name in the File As field. **H**

- To finish for one day, click **Save And Close**.
  This returns you to the main Outlook screen. When you come back to Outlook the next day you can go straight to the New Contacts icon and start adding more contacts.

- When you have entered all your contacts, (ensuring you have entered data for those items you created as User-defined Fields under the All Fields tab) finish by clicking **Save And Close**.

Hint: click the drop down arrow to the right of the File As field. If you have entered 'Mr Peter Jones' in the Name field and 'ABC Limited' in the Company field you will see the following entries in the File As drop down list:
– Jones, Peter
– Mr Peter Jones
– ABC Limited
– Jones Peter (ABC Limited)
– ABC Limited (Jones, Peter).
If you click on the last one, ABC Limited (Jones, Peter), you will be able to search (using Find) for either ABC or Jones. You will also get several contacts at the same organisation filed consecutively if you should know more than one person at an organisation.

IMPORTING NAMES AND ADDRESSES FROM OLD SYSTEMS

Names and addresses (and other fields that correspond to Outlook fields eg telephone number) can be imported to Outlook as long as they are in one of a number of standard formats. These formats include CSV (comma separated values), Microsoft Access, Microsoft Excel, Microsoft Schedule+ and Lotus Organiser. (For ease of importing data, ensure that the first record contains column headings, for instance the first line of an Excel spreadsheet). You import a file as follows:

1 When on the main Outlook screen, go to the **File menu** and click **Import And Export**.
You will see the Import and Export Wizard.

2 In the Choose An Action To Perform list, highlight **Import From Another Program or File** and click **Next**.
You then see the Select File Type To Import From list.

3 Highlight the type of file that contains your names and addresses and click **Next**.
You will then be asked the name of your file to import.

4 Type in the name of your file (or use the **Browse** button to find it). Leave Options defaulted to allow duplicates to be created and click **Next**.
You will be asked to Select destination folder.

5 Highlight **Contacts** and click **Next**.

6 On the next screen click the **Map Custom Fields** button.
This gives you a list on the left-hand side of all the fields that can be imported from your file and all the Outlook fields on the right-hand side.

7 Drag the fields you want imported from the **left-hand box** on top of the appropriate fields in the **right-hand box**.
(Note that you have to open up the **Name** and **Business Address** in the right-hand box by clicking the '+' sign before you can do this.)

8 As you drag fields across you will see the names of your fields appear in the Mapped From column.

9 When you have completed this 'mapping' procedure, click **OK**.

10 Click **Finish**.

The system then imports the file and returns you to the main Outlook screen where all the imported names and addresses will now appear.

FINDING CONTACT RECORDS

By now you will probably have several hundred names and addresses on your database (either entered manually or imported from another system) and you will want to be able to find records quickly. As with all Windows functions there is more than one way to do this. You can use:

- the horizontal scroll bar and the letter buttons on the main Outlook window **W** or
- the Find icon near the right-hand end of the Task bar (and also in the Tools menu).

Using the scroll bar

1 Click the **left and right arrows** to move forwards or backwards one page at a time.

2 Drag the **button on the bar** to any position.
If you have several thousand names in you database and you drag the button a long way along the bar then you may have to wait a second or two for the system to display the appropriate records.

3 Click one of the **letter buttons** on the right-hand side.
This takes you to the first contact that starts with that letter.

4 When you can see the contact you want, double click anywhere in its detail area and the complete contact record will appear.

Using the Find icon

1 Click **Find** to bring up a Find window which is very powerful. You can use a simple Find by typing any word into the Look For box and clicking **Find Now** or you can click **Advanced Find** to bring up the Advanced Find window.
There are three tabs in this window – Contacts, More Choices and Advanced:

- in the Contacts tab you can search for words or parts of words anywhere in your contacts database;
- in the More Choices tab you can search for contacts belonging to one or more Categories;
- in the Advanced tab you can search for specific values of any field in the database. This one is useful because you

Warning: This assumes that your Current View is Address Cards or Detailed Address Cards. If you don't see the words 'Address Cards' or 'Detailed Address Cards' in a Task Bar, then click the drop-down arrow in the Current View box and select one of these views.

can have several search criteria in the one Find operation and you can also search for fields that are blank (empty) or do not contain a specified value.

2 To search using any of the tabs, click **Find Now**.
This brings up a list of all contacts who match the criteria you have specified.

3 Double click on any of these contacts to take you straight to their records.

4 To return to the Find list, click **Save And Close**. Alternatively, click the **up arrow** if you are already looking at the record of the first contact in the list, and the **down arrow** if you are already looking at the last contact in the list.

VIEWING CONTACT RECORDS

Going back to the main Outlook Contacts screen, ie by closing the Find window, there is a drop down box on the Outlook Task bar called the Current View. This defines the data you see on each contact initially without going into the detailed record with its four tabs (or more if you created your own). You can experiment with these but the most useful are Address Cards (which is the default and which you are probably looking at right now), Detailed Address Cards and Phone List. This can be changed at any time to best suit what you are doing by simply clicking the drop down arrow and then highlighting and clicking the view you want, for instance Phone List.

Getting ready to use Excel

An Excel spreadsheet can be used to record and analyse income from appeals. Although we haven't yet done a mailing, we should set up the spreadsheet first so that our database is complete. Before we can do this we need to export details of our contacts to Excel:

1 When on the main Outlook screen, go to the **File menu** and click **Import And Export**.
You will see the Import and Export Wizard.

2 In the Choose An Action To Perform list, Highlight **Export To A File** and click **Next**.
You then see the Create A File Of Type list.

3 Highlight **Microsoft Excel** and click **Next**.
You then see the Select Folder To Export From list.

Note: you may want to use the **Browse** button here to choose a folder in which to save the file. The My Documents folder is a good place to put all your working files like this one.

Suggestion: use Last Name, First Name, Company and Postcode – this caters for individuals and organisations alike. Note that you have to open up the Name and Business Address by clicking the '+' sign before you can do this.

Hint: open Name and Business Address group fields up and take all the individual fields across separately. It will make life easier later on.

4 Highlight **Contacts** (we'll come back to this later when we talk about and use folders and subfolders) and click **Next**.

5 Type a name you will remember into the **Save Exported File As** box and click **Next**.
(Suggestion for name: ContactsGifts.) **N**

6 On the next screen click the **Map Custom Fields** button. This gives you a list on the left-hand side of all the fields that can be exported and the ones you have chosen to export on the right-hand side. It defaults to exporting everything.

7 Click the **Clear Map** button.

8 Drag the fields you want exported from the **left-hand box** to the **right-hand box**. **S**

There are two important issues here:

– take enough items so that you can uniquely identify the contacts in Excel;
– if you want the flexibility provided by using Excel for sending thank you letters (ie you want to include the donation amount in thank you letters automatically), then drag across the whole Name and Address. **H**

9 When you have completed this mapping procedure, click **OK**.

10 Click **Finish**.

The system then exports the file and returns you to the main Outlook screen.

Setting up Excel to record and analyse income

IMPORTING THE CONTACT DETAILS

■ Start Excel via the Office Task Bar, Desktop Shortcut or Start button.

■ Open the file you exported (called ContactsGifts if you followed the suggestion above).
If you did not specify a directory to put it into when you named the file in the Export function, then you will probably find it in the main Windows directory.

■ You will find that the export has brought across the field names and put them in the first row. This is essential for later mail merging and for identifying the data in each column. You can change these names if you like at this stage.

CREATING COLUMNS FOR INCOME INFORMATION

1 Go to the first blank column, ie column E if you only imported Last Name, First Name, Company and Postcode.

2 Start entering column headings for the income information you intend to store.
For example you might put Appeal1 Date in cell E1, Appeal1 Amount in cell F1, Appeal2 Date in cell G1, Appeal2 Amount in cell H1 etc.

3 Format the date and amount columns for ease of viewing and for use in mail merge.
For example, to enter the date information for the above, click **E** (to select the whole column), then click **Format**, then click **Cells**, then click **Date**, then click whichever format of date you prefer. Repeat for column G.

4 To enter amount information, click **F**, then click **Format**, then click **Cells**, then click **Currency**, then click whichever format of numbers you prefer. **S**

5 Repeat for column H.

Suggestion: use two decimal places and include the 'f' currency symbol because you can merge it directly into a standard thank you letter.

Figure 7 At this stage a simple contacts spreadsheet should look like this

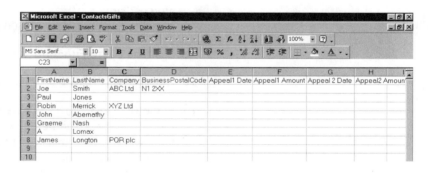

CREATING SIMPLE STATISTICS

To help monitor the success of your campaign you can create some simple but useful formulae to work out:

- the total value of donations for each appeal using the Excel SUM function;
- the number of donations for each appeal using the Excel COUNT function;
- the average donation value for each appeal using the Excel AVERAGE function.

To do this:

1 Go to a cell three below the last contact line in the first Amount column.

(In the example above, if we had 1,500 contacts then it would be cell F1504 because the first line is headings.)

2 Click the **Paste Function** (fx) icon on the Task bar.

3 Highlight **SUM** and click **OK**.

4 In the SUM window type **F2:F9999** (where 9999 equals the number of contacts plus 3, which is 1503 in our case) in the box labelled Number1 and click **OK**.
Move to the cell below (F1505 in our case).

5 Click the **Paste Function** (fx) icon on the Task bar.

6 Highlight **COUNT** and click **OK**.

7 In the COUNT window type **F2:F9999** (1503 in our case) in the box labelled Number1 and click **OK**.

8 With the average cell (F1505 in our example) still highlighted, click **Format**, click **Cells**, click **Number**, change the decimal places to 0 and click **OK**.
(If you do not do this, the average will have two decimal places and a '£' sign in front because of the column format we created earlier.)
Move to the cell below (F1506 in our example).

9 Click the **Paste Function** (fx) icon on the Task bar.

10 Highlight **AVERAGE** and click **OK**.

11 In the AVERAGE window type **F2:F9999** (1503 in our case) in the box labelled Number1 and click **OK**.
(Ignore '#DIV/0!' – this is just telling you that you are trying to divide something by zero and it will disappear as soon as you start entering income into your spreadsheet.)

12 Type 'Total income to date', 'Number of donations' and 'Average donation value' into appropriate cells (C1504, C1505, C1506 in our example).

13 Later on when you are ready to start entering income for Appeal2 you can copy the statistics cells from Appeal1 to the appropriate cells for Appeal2 but don't do it yet!

Creating a summary worksheet

For ease of viewing and for ease of analysis later on we need to move the SUM, COUNT and AVERAGE lines to another spreadsheet (or 'worksheet') summarising the appeal proceeds:

1 Create a summary worksheet as follows:

- click Menu item **Insert**;
- click **Worksheet** and a new worksheet will appear;
- double click the worksheet tab called **Sheet1** and overtype Sheet1 with **Summary**.
  You now have two tabs, one labelled Contacts and one labelled Summary.

2 Copy the heading line from the contacts spreadsheet to the summary worksheet:

- click the **Contacts worksheet tab**
- click **1** to select row one;
- click the **Copy** icon;
- click the **Summary worksheet tab** you created;
- click on **1** to select row one;
- click the **Paste** icon.

3 Move the summary lines from the contacts spreadsheet to the summary worksheet:

- select the **three summary lines** by depressing the left mouse button on the row number of the Total To-date row (1504 in our example);
- drag the mouse down two lines and release it (1506 in our example);
- click the **Cut** icon;
- click the **Summary worksheet tab** you created;
- select row numbers 3, 4 and 5;
- click the **Paste** icon.

The rows with their calculations have now moved to the Summary tab.

4 The SUM, COUNT and AVERAGE functions will still work when you enter amounts into the appropriate cells in the contacts spreadsheet. You can see the figures at any time from wherever you are in your contacts spreadsheet with a single click of the mouse on the Summary tab. You can now do things like sort your rows in the Contacts worksheet on any criteria you like and the calculations do not get corrupted.

5 Click the **Save** icon to save the spreadsheet, say as, ContactsGifts.

Figure 8 The Summary tab of the spreadsheet should look like this

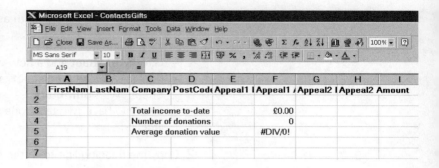

	A	B	C	D	E	F	G	H	I
1	FirstNam	LastNam	Company	PostCode	Appeal1 I	Appeal1 /	Appeal2 I	Appeal2 Amount	
2									
3			Total income to-date			£0.00			
4			Number of donations			0			
5			Average donation value			#DIV/0!			
6									
7									

You might do the above differently or choose to do different calculations. The beauty of this method is that every time you input an income amount then the SUM, COUNT and AVERAGE figures are recalculated immediately. We will extend these statistics in the next chapter when we discuss reports (see page 54).

Chapter summary

You have now learnt what is contained within Outlook, you have set up the additional data fields that you need, you have created all your contacts and you have set up a spreadsheet to accept data on income and provide a simple analysis. You are now in a position to start using the database by recording the communications you have with your contacts, preparing mailshots and recording income.

CHAPTER 4

Using a simple fundraising database

Having put all the pieces in place for your database, you are ready to start using it. The database will enable you to record communications with people, mail people, record income from people, analyse the income and draw conclusions on the success (or otherwise) of your fundraising campaigns. This chapter gives very detailed, step by step instructions for using the database you have created.

Recording communications with contacts

As discussed earlier, you can use the Outlook Journal to note the dates you speak to contacts in your database, when you send them a letter or other communication and brief note of the contents. The Journal will prove invaluable for campaigns which do not involve mass mailing eg corporate fundraising, trust fundraising and big-gift fundraising. To create entries in the Journal:

1 Find your contact record as described in Chapter 3 (see page 35).

2 Click the **Actions** menu item.

3 The Journal Entry window appears. Click the **New Journal Entry for Contact** item.

4 Select the appropriate **Entry Type** from the list.

5 Type any notes into the large box.

6 Click **Save** and **Close**.

Hint: The Subject box defaults to the Contact's name. Overtype this with something descriptive. Then when you display the Journal List for the contact, it will be more meaningful. (See Figure 3 on page 21.)

You can also use the Journal to record future actions. For instance, if you are applying to a grant-making trust, create a Journal item for the date when you have to send off the application letter. You can then use the Find function to find these records on or before the due date as follows: Find icon, Advanced Find, Look For (Journal Entries), Journal Entries tab, Time (Starts), then select Next Month for example from the list and click Find Now.

Mailing

MAILING EVERYONE ON THE DATABASE

This is simplicity itself. You do not even have to open Outlook. There are many ways to do this, but here is one of the easiest (although the list below is long, every step is simple and you can follow it with ease):

1 Open **Word** (if you have a template for letters, use that).

2 Type your letter.
Leave name and address blank, start with the date, do not insert a name after the salutation 'Dear', then type your letter text.

3 Click **Tools**, then click **Mail Merge**.
The Mail Merge Helper pops up. The first item is Main Document with a Create button under it.

4 Click **Create**.
You get a choice of Form Letters, Mailing Labels, Envelopes and Catalog.

5 Click **Form Letters**.
You get a choice of Active Window or New Main Document.

6 Click **Active Window**.
The system fills in the Merge Type you have selected and the name of the document (you haven't given it a name yet so it probably says Document 1) below the Create button and gives you a new button called Edit.

7 Under Data Source click the **Get Data** button.
You get a choice of Create Data Source, Open Data Source, Use Address Book and Header Options.

8 Click **Use Address Book**.
You will then get a window saying Choose Address Book with a list in it. There may be several items in this list but the first one is Outlook Address Book.

9 Highlight **Outlook Address Book** (it probably is already) and click **OK**.
You then get the message 'Word found no merge fields in your main document'. Don't worry about it because we are going to put them into the document now. **N**

10 Click the **Edit Main Document** button.
You will now see two new items have appeared on a Task bar: Insert Merge Field and Insert Word Field.

Note: If you created sub-folders under your Outlook Contacts folder (say for Individuals and for Organisations) you will first of all get a window appearing which asks you to select the folder you want to use in the mail merge.

11 Position your cursor to where you want your name and address to be entered and click **Insert Merge Field**.
This gives you a list of all the Outlook fields starting with Courtesy Title, First Name, etc. (Note that 'Courtesy Title' means Mr, Mrs etc and 'Title' means job title.)

12 Click **Courtesy Title** and <<Courtesy Title>> pops into your document.

13 Type a space (or the First Name will be immediately next to the Title), click Insert **Merge Field** and click **First Name**.

14 Carry on through all the fields that you need.
You may follow a sequence such as this: space, Insert Merge Field, Last Name, Insert Merge Field, Generation, Enter (or however you choose to start a new line), Insert Merge Field, Title, Enter, Insert Merge Field, Company, Enter, Insert Merge Field, Postal Address.

15 If you want to insert the full address including, street, town, county and postcode, select **Postal Address**.
You can also select any item from the address separately if you wish.

16 You can then position the cursor to one space beyond the salutation 'Dear', click **Insert Merge Field** and click **First Name**.
This may cause you a problem as you probably don't have all the first names of your contacts. To overcome this you need a salutation field, but Outlook doesn't give you one and there are no wholly satisfactory ways of getting round this. Although inserting an informal salutation is difficult, inserting a formal one is easy. All you have to do is insert the Courtesy Title and the Surname.

17 Having inserted all the Merge fields you need into your letter, go back to the Mail Merge Helper by either clicking **Tools** and then **Mail Merge** or clicking the **Mail Merge Helper** icon you will now find on the same line as the Insert Merge Field button. Under the Merge button you will see the following default options: Suppress Blank Lines in Addresses and Merge to New Document.

18 Click **Merge**.
You get the Merge window displayed. The Merge to field is set to New Document (there is an option to send it direct to the printer but that's not a very good idea because you cannot check the letters first).

19 Click the **Merge** button and in a few seconds the first of your mail-merged letters appears on the screen.

20 You can then check them, alter any if you wish, print them and save them if you wish.

21 Now click **Window** on the Menu bar and click **Document 1** (assuming this is your Form Letter) to switch to your form letter and **Save** it.
You can then make use of this letter again for another mail merge.

The operation is now complete.

MAILING A SELECTED GROUP OF CONTACTS ON THE DATABASE

In order to target your mailing to a particular group of supporters, you can pick out selected groups (or sub-sets) of contacts to receive your letter. This can be done by creating a Filter during the mail merge using the Query Options button, which you find in Mail Merge Helper under Merge Data With The Document. This is of little value, however, unless you are going to filter on an address feature such as Town/City or County because useful fields, such as Category, are not accessible from the Mail Merge Helper. So let's look at how we can create a mailing to be sent to all contacts of a specific Category. We are going to copy (always copy, never move) all contacts we want in our small mailing to a subfolder which we will then use in a Word mail merge.

1 Go into Outlook and click on the **Contacts** icon.

2 Click **File** on the Menu bar. Highlight **Folder**. Click **New Folder**.

3 Type the name of your subfolder, say VIPs, in the **Name box**.

4 Leave the Folder Contains box set to Contact Items and click **OK**.

5 If the Folder List is showing on the screen, you will see that a subfolder called VIPs has appeared under Contacts.

6 If the Folder List isn't showing, then click the **Folder List** icon on the Task bar (it is immediately to the left of the Printer icon). This will show you a list of all Outlook folders. If you don't see VIPs then you will see Contacts with a '+' sign in front of it. Click **+** to reveal the subfolders and VIPs should be there.

7 Click **VIPs**.
You will see the message 'There are no items to show in this view. Double click here to create a new contact'.

8 Don't double click there, instead click **Contacts**.
If you want to select a single contact to copy to the subfolder then:

- find the contact and double click on the record so you can check it is the right one;
- click **File** on the Menu bar;
- click **Copy To Folder**;
- highlight **VIPs** and click **OK**;
- click **Save And Close** to take you back to the main Contacts screen;
- Click **VIPs** from the folder list (which should still be showing – click the Folder List icon if it isn't).

You should now see the Address Card of one contact on the screen. You can now continue to add other contacts in the same way.

9 To select all the contacts of a particular category to copy to the subfolder then:

- make sure that the Contacts Folder is highlighted;
- click the **Find** icon on the Task bar;
- click **Advanced Find**;
- click the **More Choices** tab;
- click **Categories**;
- click **VIP** (or any other required Category) – note that this action puts a tick in the box;
- click **OK**;
- click **Find Now** and a list of contacts within that category will appear in the bottom of the Find Contacts box;
- click anywhere on the line of any one of the contacts you found (otherwise the next bit doesn't work);
- click **Edit** on the Menu bar of the Advanced Find window to get a drop down list of options;
- click **Select All** (all the contacts in the list should go blue);
- click **Edit** (again);
- click **Copy To Folder**;
- highlight **VIPs** and click **OK**;
- close the Find box to return to the main Contacts screen;
- click **VIPs** from the folder list (which should still be showing – click the **Folder List** icon if it isn't) and you should now see the Address Cards of all the contacts who have VIP as one of their categories. **N**

Note: you can select multiple Categories in the one Find if you wish. You can also use any of the other Find options to select groups of contacts and copy them to a subfolder in the same way.

10 When you have all the contacts you want in your subfolder, go into Word and create your form letter as before, this time selecting VIPs instead of Contacts when you get your list of Folders displayed.

Recording income

INCOME FROM KNOWN CONTACTS

When the money starts flowing in from the mailings you have done, you can record the income as follows:

1 Go into the Excel spreadsheet you created earlier (we called it ContactsGifts).

2 Find the contact from whom you have received a cheque. (Use the **Scroll bar** or **page down** if your database is not too big, ie less than 1,000 records, or use the **Find** function, which is on the Edit Menu, if you have more records.)

3 To avoid confusion when scrolling down or across, it is advisable to fix the heading line and the columns that identify the contacts. To do this:

- make sure that cell A1 is visible in the left-hand corner of the worksheet;
- click on **any cell** except one in line 1 or column 1 (in fact in our example it would be best to click on cell E2);
- click **Window** on the Menu bar;
- click **Split** and you will see a vertical line and a horizontal line drawn across your worksheet. If the horizontal line is immediately underneath the heading and the vertical line is immediately to the right of the Postcode then fine. If not, then drag them until they are;
- click **Window** and click **Freeze Panes**.

Now, wherever you move in the worksheet, you will always see your column headings (to ensure that you always get the amount, date etc, into the right columns) and you will always see the Surname, First Name, Company and Postcode of your contacts (to ensure that you always put the amount, date etc against the right contact).

4 Enter the amount received into the **appropriate cell** (and the date and any other items you decided to store).

5 Continue to find each contact and enter amounts and any other data against the appropriate Appeal.

6 Click the **Summary** worksheet tab to see the latest total to date, number of donations and average donation value.

INCOME FROM ANONYMOUS DONORS

Dealing with a few donations

The obvious way of handling anonymous donations is to record each one on a separate row of the main Contacts worksheet. This means inserting a new row 2 for the first anonymous donation. This has a peculiar side-effect. Inserting a new row 2 into the Contacts worksheet alters the formulae on the Summary worksheet to start at row 3 instead of row 2. You will have to select cell F3 (total income to date) on the Summary worksheet and change F3 to F2 in the formula. Similarly change the F3 to F2 in the formulae in cells F4 (number of donations) and F5 (average donation value). You then insert a new row 3 for every subsequent anonymous donation. To ensure that these lines are always sorted to the same place, type 'aaa' into First Name, Company and Postcode and type 'aanon1', 'aanon2' etc into the Surname of successive anonymous donation lines.

Large numbers of donations

This is fine unless you get a lot of anonymous donations and you have pages of them listed before your known Contacts. In this case you could:

Warning: Remember to change F3 to F2 in every formula on the summary worksheet.

1 Create a single line on your Contacts worksheet for the anonymous donor (click anywhere on line 2, click **Insert** (on the Menu bar), click **Row**. **W**

2 For your second anonymous donation, create another worksheet (click **Insert**, click **Worksheet**, double click the **sheet name** and type in 'Anonymous Donations').

3 For simplicity, copy the heading line from the Contacts worksheet to the new worksheet.
You don't actually need columns A to D in this example but it is easier to keep them in and simply re-size them to make them small. The easiest way to re-size column A for example is to hover the mouse over the vertical column marker to the right of the letter A (the cursor should turn into a vertical bar with arrows pointing left and right) and drag the line to the left.

4 Format the Amount columns (click **F** to select the whole column F, click **Format**, click **Cells**, click **Currency**, ensure that Decimal places = '2' and Symbol = '£', click **OK**, repeat for every other amount column).

5 Type **0** into cell F20 and into every other Amount cell across line 20.

6 Create a total for all Appeals on line 21. One way to do this is: click **cell F21**, click the **Paste Function** icon (fx), click **SUM**, click **OK**, type **F2:F20** into Number1 box, click **OK**, then copy cell F21 to every other amount cell across line 21 (click on **F21**, click **Copy** icon, click on **H21**, click **Paste** icon, click **J21**, click **Paste** icon etc).

7 Now transfer this total line to the main Contacts worksheet (click **21** to select the entire line), click **Cut**, click the **Contacts** tab, click **2** (to select the line you added for the anonymous donor), click **Paste**.

8 Ensure that this line is always sorted to the same place by typing 'aaanonymous' in Surname and typing 'aaa' into First Name, Company and Postcode.

9 Now when you get an anonymous donation you enter it in the appropriate Appeal Amount column in the Anonymous Donations worksheet starting on line 2. Enter the second anonymous donation on line 3 and so on.

10 When you get down to line 20 where we have the zero, click on the **zero**, click **Insert**, click **Row** and repeat Insert and Row to create as many new lines as you need. This will automatically update the formula (and consequently the totals) on the Contacts worksheet. This is not very elegant and you have to remember to do it, but it is one of the little compromises you have to make when you do a job like this without a proper database. The point is that it works!

The side-effect of this will be that all anonymous donations are now considered to be a single donation for the purposes of Number of Donations and Average Donation Value on the Summary worksheet. (There are ways around this but it is easier to live with it.)

NON-INCOME INFORMATION

When you receive donations you will often receive letters from supporters containing other information that you need to record. This could be a change of address, a complaint about the mailing, an indication of the supporter's specific interests or details of a friend or relative who you should put on your database. You can save all these up to deal with after you have recorded all the income or you can open Outlook as well as Excel and flick back and forth between the two windows as you deal with each cheque and/or letter.

Sending thank you letters

There are different ways of approaching this depending on the volume of letters you have to produce each day. If you send only a few letters it is probably easiest to produce them one at a time from Word. If you have a larger number to deal with and you don't want to include in the letter text the exact amount the supporter gave (or you are happy to add this amount individually to each letter before it is printed), then you can do a mail merge from Outlook. If there are a larger number of records to produce and you want the donation amount to be included automatically, then a mail merge from Excel is a suitable method.

ONE AT A TIME USING WORD

If you only get one or two cheques in a day then this is probably the easiest way to create a thank you letter.

1 Go into Word and create the standard thank you letter text.

2 Click **Tools** and click **Letter Wizard**.
The Letter Wizard appears with four tabs: Letter Format, Recipient Info, Other Elements and Sender Info. (You can experiment with all of these but the only one we will consider is Recipient Info).

3 Click the **Recipient Info** tab, then click the **picture of an open book** beside the words Click Here To Use Address Book.
This brings up the Select Names box and Contacts appears in the box at the top.

4 Click the **down arrow** beside this box.
You get a list of all the folders that contain contacts.

5 Click the folder that contains your contacts, probably **Contacts**.
A list of contacts appears in the large box with a scroll bar. Strangely, what you get is the list of contacts sorted by First Name rather than Surname, or the Company Name if you entered no individual's name.

Hint: Use Find to Search for Surnames.

6 You can search for a contact by entering a name in the Type Name Or Select From List field or by using the scroll bar or by clicking the Find button to find names containing words or parts of words. **H**
(You can click the Properties button to check that you have got the right contact before actually selecting it. This brings up the contact's Outlook record. Check it and close the record.)

7 Highlight the **contact name** you want from the list and click **OK**.
The name and address of the contact will appear in the Recipient's Name and Delivery Address boxes.

8 Select the type of **Salutation** you want.

9 Click **OK**.
The name, address and salutation appear in the letter.

A less sophisticated but easier method is to have Outlook open as well as Word, write your letter in Word, switch to Outlook, find your Contact, copy and paste the Name from Outlook to your letter and then copy and paste the Address from Outlook to your letter. This is simple and unsophisticated but it works.

DEALING WITH MORE LETTERS – MAIL MERGE FROM OUTLOOK

If you have quite a few donations and you want to send the same thank you letter to everyone, then:

1 Open Outlook and click on the **Contacts** icon.

2 Click **File**, click **Folder**, click **New Folder**.

3 Type 'Today's Thank You Letters ' into the Name field.

4 Leave the Folder Contains field set to Contact Items and click **OK**.

5 If the Folder List is not showing, then click the **Folder List** icon to see that the subfolder was created properly.

6 Now click the **Contacts folder** and find the first contact you want to thank and open the **Outlook record** for this contact.

7 Click **File** and click **Copy To Folder**.

8 Highlight **Today's Thank You Letters** and click **OK**.

9 Close the contact record.

10 Repeat for all other contacts who sent donations.

11 When you have finished copying all the contact records to the Today's Thank You Letters subfolder, click this subfolder (click the **Folder List** icon first if the folder list is not visible) and check that all the names you expected are in the folder.

12 Open Word, create your thank you letter and do a mail merge as described before, but this time choose the Today's Thank

You Letters subfolder as the Data Source.
If you want to include the actual amount that each contact has given into each thank you letter, you will have to enter this after you have done the merge but before you print the letters.

13 When you have printed your thank you letters go back to Outlook and the Today's Thank You Letters subfolder.

14 To clear the Today's Thank You Letters subfolder so that it is ready for tomorrow, highlight each **Address Card** in turn and click the **Delete** icon. (Make absolutely sure you are looking at the Today's Thank You Letters subfolder first.)

15 Continue to do this until you see the words 'There are no more items to show in this view'.
This is a bit tedious but the alternative is to delete the entire subfolder which means that you would have to create it again the next day – not that this is very difficult. (You might think that clicking Edit, Select All and Delete would simply delete all the contacts from the subfolder and leave the empty subfolder there but unfortunately it deletes the subfolder as well!)

DEALING WITH MORE LETTERS – MAIL MERGE FROM EXCEL

If you have a lot of thank you letters to send on one day and you also want to include automatically into each letter the actual amount received, you can do a mail merge from Excel. To use this method you will need to have exported the entire name and address from Outlook to Excel when you set up your ContactsGifts spreadsheet in the first place (see Chapter 3, page 37). Once this has been done, follow these steps:

1 Open the **ContactsGifts spreadsheet**.

2 Open a **new spreadsheet**.

3 Copy the **heading line** from ContactsGifts to the new spreadsheet.

4 One at a time, copy the row for each contact who has given you money, and to whom you wish to send a thank you letter, to the new spreadsheet.

5 Save the **spreadsheet** as, say, 'TodaysGifts'.

6 Go into Word and continue as before with a mail merge (ie Tools, Mail Merge, Main Document, Create, Active Window) but this time when you get to the Data Source section in the Mail Merge Helper, select **Open Data Source** instead of Use Address Book.

This will give you the Open screen which you will have seen many times before in Word.

7 Select **MS Excel Worksheet** from the drop down Files of Type list, and find your **TodaysGifts file**.
When you have opened the file you will get a Microsoft Excel box with Entire Spreadsheet highlighted.

8 Click **OK**.
The Mail Merge Helper then continues with 'Word found no merge fields in your main document'.

9 Click **Edit Main Document**.
You will then see the Insert Merge Field and Insert Word Field buttons on a Task bar.

10 Click **Insert Merge Field** to see all the columns of the spreadsheet including the Amount you wish to thank people for.

11 Insert the name and address and the amount in the appropriate places in the letter and carry out a mail merge as before.

12 Edit the **letters** if necessary.

13 Print the **letters**.

14 Save the **standard letter** so you can use it again.

15 Go back to the **TodaysGifts spreadsheet** and delete every line except the first (the heading line) ready for the next day.

Analysing income

Having completed your mailing and received donations in response, you will want to consider which types of income analysis will be useful to you. From the way we have set up the spreadsheet, for each appeal you already have: a running total, the total number of donations and the average donation value. Below we show how to create two other useful reports in a very few minutes. The first is a 'top donors' report containing details of who has given the most money. The second is a 'response analysis' report which adds cost-related figures and a calculation of return on investment to the response totals and average figures already in the spreadsheet.

TOP DONORS REPORT

To see your best donors for any appeal you simply:

1 Open the **ContactsGifts spreadsheet**.
It is probably best to save the spreadsheet under a different name, eg 'TopDonors' so that nothing you do affects the original information.

2 Click the **Contacts** tab.

3 Delete all columns relating to other appeals ie just keep the name and address columns and the columns for this appeal. To delete a single column you can: click the column letter (the whole column is then highlighted), click **Edit** and click **Delete**. To delete several adjacent columns you can drag the cursor across all the column letters (each column is highlighted as you drag), click **Edit** and click **Delete**.

4 For the sake of simplicity, delete the heading row.

5 Put the cursor in any cell of the amount column for this appeal and click the **Sort Descending** icon (the Z over A with a down arrow).
This sorts your rows from the largest donation to the smallest.

6 Insert some heading lines and print, say, the top 10 lines direct from Excel or select the top 10 lines and copy them into a Word report.

7 You can then go back to Outlook and set these people to be in Category Key Customer, VIP or whatever high value donor category you have.
It will then be easy to single them out for special treatment, such as putting them in a separate subfolder and sending them different letters.

RESPONSE ANALYSIS

You can easily extend the simple statistics on the Summary tab of your ContactsGifts spreadsheet to work out response rates, costs per mailing, costs per response and return on investment.

- You need two additional pieces of information:

  - the number of letters sent (or number of people phoned if it was a telephone campaign);
  - the total cost of the campaign/appeal.

- Add these under the average donation values on the worksheet.

- If you used the same example as described in Chapter 3 then type 'Number Mailed' into cell C6 and 'Appeal Cost' into cell C7.

- You can then create simple formulae for working out response rates and costs:

  - type headings for these in column C (eg 'response rate' in cell C8, 'cost per mailing' in cell C9, 'cost per response' in cell C10 and 'return on investment' in cell C11);
  - calculate the formulae (see below) in column F;
  - copy these formulae to the other amount columns (see page 57).

To work out the response rate, divide the number of donations by the number mailed and express it as a percentage. One way to calculate this is:

1 Click on **cell F8**.

2 Click the '=' sign on the bar above the column letters.

3 Type **F4/F6** into the box beside the '=' sign and press **Enter**.

4 Click on **cell F8** again.

5 Click **Format**, click **Cells**, on the Number tab click **Percentage**, ensure that Decimal Places is set to 2, click **OK**.

To work out cost per mailing divide your appeal cost by the number mailed (F7/F6); for cost per response divide your appeal cost by the number of donations (F7/F4); and for a return on investment figure, divide your total income by your appeal cost expressed as a percentage (F3/F7). (Use the Format menu to get the £ signs, % signs and decimal places right if necessary.)

Do not copy the cells you have created to the corresponding cells for other appeals yet because you will end up with lots of error messages.

After you have completed all your calculations, remember to save the spreadsheet.

You can edit your spreadsheet, to make the information more suitable for presentation to others in your organisation or elsewhere. For example you can delete columns A, B, and D, alter the headings to be more meaningful and re-size columns E, G, I, K etc to make them small. Do remember not to delete the original columns E, G, I, K etc as if you do, your statistics for Appeal2, Appeal3, Appeal4 etc will not be correct.

Figure 9 This is an example of a simple response analysis as defined above

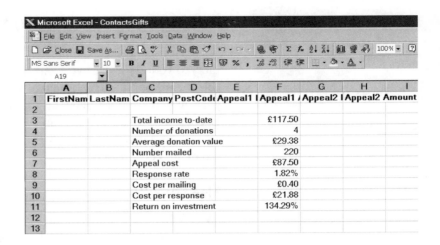

	A	B	C	D	E	F	G	H	I
1	FirstNam	LastNam	Company	PostCode	Appeal1 I	Appeal1 /	Appeal2 I	Appeal2	Amount
2									
3			Total income to-date			£117.50			
4			Number of donations			4			
5			Average donation value			£29.38			
6			Number mailed			220			
7			Appeal cost			£87.50			
8			Response rate			1.82%			
9			Cost per mailing			£0.40			
10			Cost per response			£21.88			
11			Return on investment			134.29%			
12									
13									

The Summary worksheet can now be printed directly or copied to Word for formatting and printing.

When you are ready to start entering income for Appeal2 in the Contacts tab of this spreadsheet then:

1 Select the **Summary** tab.

2 Highlight cells **C3 to C11** (if you deleted the original columns A, B and D, or cells F3 to F11 if you didn't).

3 Copy them to cells **E3 to E11** (or H3 to H11 if you didn't delete columns A, B and D).

4 Fill in the correct values for Number mailed – **E6** (or H6) and Appeal cost – **E7** (or H7).

All the statistics will now be calculated for Appeal2. This process can be repeated for Appeal3, Appeal4 etc.

OTHER REPORTS AND CALCULATIONS

The above will provide an excellent start but you have the full power of Excel available and you can create all sorts of figures and graphs. For example, with a small amount of effort you can summarise the income items by day and print a column graph of the response rate over time. (If you have the time, try it and see if you get the normal 'bell shaped' curve.) You will be limited only by your imagination, your competence with Excel and by the fields that you can export from Outlook.

Adding new contacts to the database

Your database will not stand still. You will want to add new contacts to your database every day. But (because we are doing it on the cheap) our database is actually in two completely separate parts which are not linked: an Outlook Contacts folder and an Excel spreadsheet. There is an easy way to add new contacts and a more complicated way which tries to ensure that Outlook and Excel are kept in step.

THE EASY WAY

Open both the Contacts folder in Outlook and the ContactsGifts spreadsheet in Excel. Add each new contact to both the Contacts folder and to the ContactsGifts spreadsheet one at a time. This involves switching back and forth between Outlook and Excel but this is achieved by a single mouse click and represents no difficulty. There is, however, an element of duplication of data entry and the risks that you might forget to add the new contact to the spreadsheet, or enter something incorrectly, so that the two parts of your database are not in step.

When adding a new contact to the spreadsheet, the easiest way is to insert a new row immediately below the record for the Anonymous Donor each time. When you have finished entering new contacts for the day, then sort the spreadsheet so that it is in the same sequence as the Outlook Contacts folder. This is not essential but it makes life easier.

THE NOT SO EASY (BUT BETTER?) WAY

This section will not be in as much detail as other sections, but if you want to adopt this approach, you are probably by now fairly proficient with the programs.

1 Create a Contacts subfolder called **New Contacts**.

2 Add all new contacts to this subfolder.

3 Export this subfolder to an Excel file (called NewContacts).

4 Open both **NewContacts** and **ContactsGifts** worksheets.

5 Insert as many new rows into ContactsGifts as there are Contact rows in NewContacts.

6 Cut the rows from NewContacts and paste them into ContactsGifts.

7 Sort ContactsGifts by **Company** and **Surname**.

8 Go back to Outlook and move all the contacts in New Contacts subfolder to the main Contacts folder.
(The New Contacts subfolder will remain there empty ready for the next day.)

Chapter summary

You have now set up your database and completed a full cycle of recording contact details, mailing, recording income and analysing income. You can now go round the loop as many times as you like. Some of the actions described in this chapter will not be required on the second and subsequent cycles because various subfolders and spreadsheets are now set up and simply have to be used again or added to. If you are unhappy with some of the constraints placed on you by using Outlook and Excel and you feel confident that you can handle Access, then you may like to move on to Chapter 6.

CHAPTER 5

The beginner's database in summary

This chapter contains a summary of the detailed instructions given in the previous two chapters. Its purpose is to act as a guide for experienced Office users who do not need step by step instructions but merely need ideas as to how the system can be set up and used. You can refer back to the detailed chapters if you need to at any time because the sub-headings below are the main sub-headings used in the relevant chapter.

Creating a simple fundraising database (Chapter 3)

Your 'database' will consist of two separate and mutually exclusive parts, Microsoft Outlook and Microsoft Excel. Outlook is going to record all the basic information about your contacts and Excel is going to record all the details of the income you obtain from these contacts. The first thing you need to do is to set up both Outlook and Excel so that they record the exact information necessary to manage your fundraising campaigns.

SETTING UP OUTLOOK TO RECORD CONTACT DETAILS

Open Outlook, click the Contacts icon and familiarise yourself with the data fields provided by the system to help you select groups of contacts with whom you may wish to communicate.

Look at the Categories List and use the Master Category List function to add, delete or amend categories in order to create a category list which is more meaningful to you.

On the All Fields screen, use the User-Defined Fields in the Folder item from the Select From list in order to set up specific data items that you would like to record that are not in Outlook. These might include 'date of first contact', 'do not telephone', and 'helps with events'. You must decide what fields are essential for your organisation. Don't create too many: you will have to enter the data and keep them up to date. Only create the fields that you

really need. You can add extra data items by the following procedures described in the paragraphs below.

RECORDING AND VIEWING INFORMATION ABOUT YOUR SUPPORTERS

Decide right at the start whether you want the information about
all your contacts to be together in a single folder: you may prefer
to separate some types of contact from others. For example, if you
want to keep details of individuals separate from those of organisations, you can do this by creating two 'subfolders'. There is a New
Folder option under File on the Menu bar. For the sake of simplicity, however, we will assume that you are going to store records
about individuals and organisations in the same folder, and file the
organisations by the organisation name.

Recording information about supporters is simply a case of entering the data and remembering to click the Save And New button
(Save And Close when you have entered the final one you create
in the day). When you have details of a lot of Contacts recorded
then finding a specific Contact is easily done by use of the letter
buttons and the scroll bar or by the very powerful Find function.
Find is an icon and is also on the Tools menu.

Before selecting a contact to view in detail, using the main
Outlook screen, you can see what different types of data you have
available, for instance address cards and a phone list. When viewing individual contact details themselves, as well as the five
standard tabs of General, Details, Activities, Certificates and All
Fields, you can design your own tab with any of the data items on
it in any sequence. If you want to play with that, it is in Forms,
Design a Form on the Tools menu, but in all probability you will
not need it.

GETTING READY TO USE EXCEL

An Excel spreadsheet can be used to record and analyse income
from appeals. To do this you first need to export details of your
contacts from Outlook to Excel. There is an Import and Export
function on the File menu on the main Outlook screen (not on
the File menu when looking at an individual contact record).
Take the option to create a Microsoft Excel file.

You can specify any pre-defined Outlook fields (not the user-
defined fields you have created) to be exported using the Map
Custom fields button. **S**

Suggestion: use Surname, First
Name, Company and Postcode –
this caters for Individuals and
Organisations alike.

Hint: Open Name and Business Address group fields and take all the individual fields across separately. It will make life easier later on.

There are two important issues here:

- Take enough items so that you can uniquely identify the contacts in Excel.
- If you want the flexibility provided by using Excel for sending thank you letters (ie you want to include the donation amount in thank you letters automatically), then drag across the whole Name and Address. **H**

SETTING UP EXCEL TO RECORD AND ANALYSE INCOME

You now have to create the spreadsheet to record details of income. Go into Excel and open the file you exported from Outlook. After the columns that were brought across from Outlook, add a series of columns for each appeal you intend to run eg Appeal1 Date, Appeal1 Amount, Appeal2 Date, Appeal2 Amount etc. Format the date and amount columns appropriately.

To create some simple statistics for the Appeal1 Amount column you can use the SUM, COUNT and AVERAGE functions. Only create these three functions for now and we will add to them later. Create a summary worksheet and move the statistics to it (or create the statistics directly on a summary worksheet).

Using a simple fundraising database (Chapter 4)

Once Outlook and Excel are set up and details of your contacts have been recorded you need procedures to be able to use the information in an effective manner. You also need to know how to keep Outlook and Excel in step with each other when adding new contacts to your database.

RECORDING COMMUNICATIONS WITH CONTACTS

You can use the Outlook Journal to note details of communications with your contacts. Past and future dates can be entered as the date of the Journal as well as today's date. The Advanced tab of the Find function can be used to search for particular Journal records.

MAILING

To mail a standard letter to everyone on your database, you create your letter in Word and use the Mail Merge function from the Tools menu. We assume that you are familiar with mail merge. The only difference from what you may have done before is the

Data Source. From Get Data in the Mail Merge Helper window you select Use Address Book. Within this you choose Outlook Address Book and select the Contacts folder (or Individuals or Organisations if you created those subfolders). You then continue as normal with inserting merge fields and finally doing the merge.

To mail a standard letter to a selected group or sub-set of contacts, you create a temporary subfolder under the Contacts folder in Outlook, copy the contacts you are mailing to this subfolder and then use that subfolder as the Data Source in a mail merge. Copying contacts to the temporary subfolder can be done one at a time or *en masse*. In the latter instance, use the Find function. When Find has found all the selected contact records, you copy them to your subfolder by using Edit, Select All, Edit (again) and Copy to Folder.

RECORDING INCOME

Income from known contacts is simply entered against the relevant contact in the spreadsheet. Use the Find function on the Edit menu if you have thousands of contacts.

Income from anonymous donors is awkward. You can insert a row into your contacts spreadsheet for each anonymous donation. (Remember to check the formulae in the summary worksheet after you have added the first anonymous donation row!) Alternatively you can insert a single row for the total of anonymous donations and create a new worksheet for recording the individual anonymous donations. The side-effect of this will be that all anonymous donations are now considered to be a single donation for the purposes of the data stored in the summary worksheet on the number of donations and average donation value.

SENDING THANK YOU LETTERS

You can create thank you letters one at a time from Word if you receive only a very few donations per day. You can use Recipient Info in the Letter Wizard to bring the name and address from Outlook rather than typing it in every time (or even have Outlook open as well as Word and insert the name and address with two simple copy and paste operations).

If you have quite a few donations you can create a Subfolder in Outlook called, say, Today's Thank You Letters, and copy into it the record of every contact from whom you received a donation today. You then use this Subfolder as the Data Source for a Word mail merge.

If you have lot of thank you letters to send and you want to include the amount of the donation in the text of each letter you can create a temporary spreadsheet and copy to it the rows of the contacts from whom you received a donation today. You then use this spreadsheet as the data source for a Word mail merge.

ANALYSING INCOME

The spreadsheet already gives you simple statistics of a running total, the number of donations and the average donation value for each appeal. An easy 'top donors' report can be produced by sorting the contacts worksheet in descending order of the Appeal Amount column and then printing (or copying to Word) the top 10, 20 or however many lines showing your best donors.

The simple statistics can easily be added to the spreadsheet in order to produce a more comprehensive response analysis. To the summary worksheet add two data items: the number of contacts mailed and the cost of the appeal. With the figures you already have you can now calculate the response rate, the cost per mailing, the cost per response and the return on investment. The summary worksheet can then be printed or copied to Word.

ADDING NEW CONTACTS TO THE DATABASE

New contacts will have to be added to both Outlook and the Excel spreadsheet. The easy way is to have Outlook and the spreadsheet open at the same time, add a contact to Outlook, switch to the spreadsheet and add a row for the contact, switch back to Outlook for the next new contact and so on. This means double entry and could be a bit tedious if you have many new contacts to include in a day.

If you do have a large number of Contacts to add you can:

1 Create a Contacts subfolder called **New Contacts**.

2 Add all new contacts to this subfolder.

3 Export this subfolder to an Excel file (called NewContacts).

4 Open both **NewContacts** and **ContactsGifts** worksheets.

5 Insert as many new rows into ContactsGifts as there are Contact rows in NewContacts.

6 Cut the rows from NewContacts and paste them into ContactsGifts.

7 Sort ContactsGifts by **Company** and **Surname**.

8 Go back to Outlook and move all the contacts in New Contacts subfolder to the main Contacts folder.
(The New Contacts subfolder will remain there empty ready for the next day.)

A more advanced database

After reading the previous section you may have decided that you do not want the inconvenience of having to keep two separate systems (Outlook and Excel) in step with each other. Or you may have decided that the Outlook and Excel methods are not suitable for your purposes. If, however, you need many more than the five tables included here – Contacts, Appeals, Gifts, Communication Log and Notes – you should consider a packaged fundraising system (see Chapter 11, page 132).

This section describes how to use a 'programming' tool, Access, to create a fundraising database that you can tailor to your exact needs. It describes how to build a simple but effective fundraising database from scratch.

Although the step by step techniques of Section 2 are used again here, you should really only attempt this section if you already have created your own database, or have set one up using Section 2 of this book, and have experimented with different facilities. Ideally you should have a basic level of familiarity with Access and you should have used and maintained one or more of the simple databases that are provided with every copy of the program.

The following four chapters explain the day to day use of the Access database to assist you in the research, strategy and monitoring phases of your fundraising cycle. Chapters 6 and 7 contain step by step instructions for creating and using the database and Chapter 8 gives summary instructions for the more confident users of computers in general and of Access in particular. Chapter 9 shows how to make the database more user-friendly.

CHAPTER 6

Creating a more advanced fundraising database

This chapter describes how to set up the database. It starts by describing the tools we will use and the way in which we will use them. There is then a breakpoint where confident Access users can skip to Chapter 8 for summary instructions or less confident users can carry on with very detailed step by step instructions on how to set up the database.

As mentioned in the introduction to this section, we will use Access first to create five tables with which to record and analyse information about your fundraising campaign:

- Contacts
- Appeals
- Gifts
- Communication Log
- Notes

These tables will then be linked together ready for use. We will then go on to create four Access forms:

- Appeals
- Contacts
- Gifts
- Contact Gifts, Communications and Notes

We need forms as well as tables for two reasons. First, the default way of entering data to an Access table is via a 'datasheet', which looks like a spreadsheet; however, forms are more attractive and provide an easier way of entering data. Second, forms are more flexible and we can combine elements of different tables on a single form; for instance we can have the name and address, as well as the contact number, on a form containing gift information. Some hints are then included on how to find your way around the database and finally the chapter gives step by step instructions on entering your data into your forms.

An integrated database?

With Access we will create an **integrated** database, which means that everything will be stored in one place, unlike the database described in Section 2 where some information was stored in Outlook and some in Excel. This means that there will be no special procedures to ensure that data is kept in step in two systems. (You may indeed decide to do calculations and produce reports and graphs using Excel but you can export the information to Excel just for the report/graph and not keep the Excel data after producing the report.) The only other tool you need for this exercise is Word for producing your mail-merged letters.

What is Access?

Many people think that Access is a database, but it isn't. It is actually a programming tool for creating a database. You do not need to be a specialist to use it: Access is a good example of bringing the world of computer programming to non-computer people. Many fundraisers have created excellent databases themselves, simply by reading the manual and spending a few hours persevering with the system to get it right. It is true that only a computer boffin will make the most effective use of a tool like Access, but mere mortals like us can create something that works, and in the long run that is all that matters.

How Access and Word are used

ACCESS

In Access we will create five linked tables which should contain all the data you need for the research, strategy, monitoring and analysis of your campaign. These will be:

- **Contacts** – name and address and other general information similar to the Contacts tab in Outlook.
- **Appeals** – general information about each appeal from which useful analysis reports can be produced.
- **Gifts** – this will record all details related to gifts including date, amount and the appeal to which the gift was given.
- **Communication Log** – this table will record details about your communications with contacts.
- **Notes** – this will be a free text area where you can record any other information about your contacts.

Clearly, the Gifts, Communication Log and Notes tables have to be linked to the Contacts table. In order to do this we will have to give each contact a unique reference number (commonly called an URN). You can get the computer to allocate this automatically. Also, each gift will be linked to a specific appeal by creating Appeal Codes.

After creating the tables we will create a set of data input forms using the Access Forms function. A suitable set of forms would be:

- **Appeals** – as with the Appeals table above, this will contain general information about each appeal from which useful analysis reports can be produced.
- **Contacts** – this contains similar information on contacts to that in the Contacts table.
- **Gifts** – this contains similar information to the Gifts table, but it is useful only if you need to enter a large number of income items in one operation.
- **Contact Gifts, Communications and Notes** – this contains the basic details of the contact, details of all their gifts, your communications with them and any notes.

WORD

Word is used for writing letters to contacts. When you are writing to groups of supporters you will use the mail merge facility to select all the names and addresses to be entered onto the letters automatically from the Access database. We will start by creating a mailing for everyone in your database. We will then see how easy it is to select smaller groups of people from your database and mail these smaller groups in the same way as the whole database. Word is also useful for producing reports when you reach the analysis stage of your campaign.

Data modelling

Data modelling is a technical term used to describe the functions of deciding what files (or tables) you want, what data items you want in these tables and how the tables are linked together. Figure 10 shows the simple model that we will use.

Note that the line with the 'crow's foot' at the end represents a 'one to many' relationship, for instance one contact may be related to many gifts, as may one appeal.

The 'one to many' concept also incorporates the possibility of a 'one to none' and a 'one to one' relationship. This allows us to have, for example, some contacts who have no gifts linked to them, some who have one gift linked to them and some who have more than one gift linked to them.

Figure 10 Data model showing the tables you need, the data to be included in the tables and how the tables will be linked together

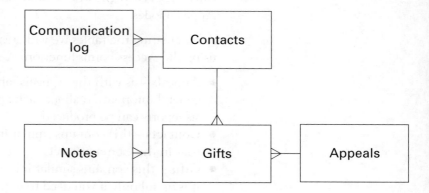

To link the data in each table, each contact's URN will be included in every relevant Communication Log record, Gift record and Notes record. As well as an URN, every Gift record will also contain the relevant Appeal Code in order to make the link between the Appeals and Gifts tables.

Are you an experienced user of Access?

If you are an experienced user of Access and do not need step by step instructions on how to use it, then move straight to Chapter 8 for a summary of how Access can be used to create a fundraising database. If you are not a confident Access user, and feel you need instructions at the level of which buttons to press and when, then carry on through this chapter and Chapter 7.

Setting up an Access database and creating your tables

STARTING ACCESS

1 Go into Access by clicking the Office Task bar icon for Access (it looks like a brass key) or by clicking **Start** and **Microsoft Access**.

2 Under the heading Create New Database Using click **Blank Access Database** and click **OK**.
(Although Microsoft has set up some simple databases under Database Wizard, they all have an American flavour and you

would need a combination of at least two of them. With a bit of effort you can set up your own, so ignore this option.)

3 To name your database, type a name into the File Name field (eg Appeal Contacts) and click the **Create** button.

4 You then get the main Access screen with seven tabs down the left hand side: Tables, Queries, Forms, Reports, Pages, Macros and Modules.

For the purposes of creating your database, you will first use the Tables tab (see below) and later you will use the Forms tab. Using the Tables tab you will create the structure and format of the data you want to store, and using the Forms tab you will create a set of input forms which you will use later for entering all the details of your contacts.

CREATING YOUR CONTACTS TABLE

One at a time you will create the five tables described earlier: Contacts, Appeals, Gifts, Communication Log and Notes. Start with the Contacts table by following the steps below.

How to set up your first field

1 Click the **Tables** tab and you will see three entries describing different ways to create a table.

2 Double click the item **Create Table in Design View**. You then get a Table window with three columns: Field Name, Data Type and Description.

3 Click in the **Field Name** space on the first blank line and key in 'Contact Number'.

4 Click in the **Data Type** space next to it (or hit the **Tab** key) and then click the **down arrow** to display a list of all the valid types of data field you can include in your table.

5 From this list click on **AutoNumber**. When you start to enter contacts to your database later, this will allocate a unique number to each new contact you add to the database. The number enables you to find the contact and can be used to link with other tables we will create later.

6 If you need to, you can then click in the **Description** space (or **Tab** to it) and type a description of the field you have created, but try to use meaningful field names and don't bother with descriptions.

7 At the bottom of the Table box some fields will have appeared under the General tab. Click where it says **No** against the heading Indexed. Click the **down arrow**. Click **Yes (No Duplicates)**.

8 You have now set up your first field.

Creating your other fields

1 Click in the next **Field Name** space and type Title.

2 The default Data Type is Text so leave it, but do go down to the General tab and change the Field Size (ie the length of the field) to, say, 10, otherwise the Title field will be 50 characters long. Do this with every text field so you don't end up with a screen full of blank spaces.

3 Continue with all the other fields you want in your Contacts table. Some suggestions follow:

– First Name (Field Size 15)
– Other Initials (Field Size 3)
– Surname (Field Size 25)
– Honours/Qualifications (Field Size 20)
– Job Title (Field Size 40)
– Organisation Name (Field Size 40)
– Address Line 1 (Field Size 40)
– Address Line 2 (Field Size 40)
– Address Line 3 (Field Size 40)
– Town (Field Size 15)
– County (Field Size 15)
– Postcode (Field Size 8)
– Salutation (Field Size 30)
– Business Telephone (Field Size 15)
– Home Telephone (Field Size 15)
– Mobile Phone (Field Size 15)
– E-mail Address (Field Size 30)
– Appeal Mailings (Data Type yes/no)
– Telephone (Data Type yes/no)
– Newsletter (Data Type yes/no)
– Raffle Tickets (Data Type yes/no)
– Christmas Card (Data Type yes/no)
– Annual Report (Data Type yes/no)
– Contact Type (Field Size 15)

Defining values for your fields

You will need to define how you wish to categorise the records in your Contacts table, for instance you may wish to categorise each of your contacts by whether they are a high value donor, an individual, a company, a school, a trust or another organisation. You created a field called Contact Type for this purpose. The Access function which enables you to define these categories is 'values'.

To define a set of valid values in the Contact Type field from which you can choose when entering new contact records:

1 Click the **Data Type** box next to Contact Type.

2 Click the **down arrow** and click **Lookup Wizard**.

3 In the Lookup Wizard box click on the text that says **'I will type in the values that I want'** and then click **Next**.

4 You can then enter all the possible valid values of the Contact Type field:

   – leave the Number of Columns set at 1;
   – click in the white space under the heading Col1 and enter your first value eg High Value Donor. Note that in doing this a second line appears;
   – hit the Tab key (or use the mouse) and enter the second value eg Individual Donor;
   – continue with all other values.

5 When you have finished, click **Next**.

6 The system asks you for a label for the Lookup Column. It defaults to your Field Name so leave it as it is and click **Finish**.

7 You are now returned to the screen where you were defining your table. If you now click the **Lookup** tab you will see a number of fields filled in with things like 'Combo Box', 'Value List' and all your Contact Type values surrounded by quotation marks.

8 You can use the same technique on any of the other fields, such as Title and County in particular, if you want to.

Defining a Primary key

A 'Primary key' describes one or more fields that will uniquely identify every record that is added to the table. A Primary key is also needed for creating links with other tables and for rapid searching. We will obviously use Contact Number as our Primary key.

- Click anywhere in the Contact Number line in the Table and click the **Primary Key** icon (it looks like a little key held vertically).
  You will find that a Key symbol appears next to the Contact Number field name.

- Click the **Save** icon (or click the **Close** button of the Table box) you will be asked to name the file, so enter **Contacts** and click **OK**.

You have now created your first Access table and it probably took you no more than fifteen minutes! (See Figure 11 and Table 2.)

If you clicked the **Close** button you will be back at the Database window with its seven tabs. If you chose to click the **Save** icon, then you will now have to click the Close button. You will see that the box now contains an additional entry called Contacts.

Figure 11 The Contacts table you create should look something like this. Note that you have to scroll up and down to see all the fields. Make sure that the 'key' symbol appears beside Contact Number before you Save

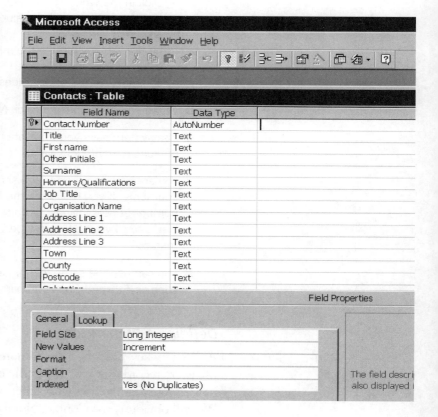

Table 2 The Contacts table you
have just created in summary
form

Contacts table

Field Name	Data Type	Field Size/Format
Contact Number	AutoNumber	Long Integer
Title	Text	10
First Name	Text	15
Other Initials	Text	3
Surname	Text	25
Honours/Qualifications	Text	20
Job Title	Text	40
Organisation Name	Text	40
Address Line 1	Text	40
Address Line 2	Text	40
Address Line 3	Text	40
Town	Text	15
County	Text	15
Postcode	Text	8
Salutation	Text	30
Business Telephone	Text	15
Home Telephone	Text	15
Mobile Phone	Text	15
E-mail Address	Text	30
Appeal Mailings	Yes/No	
Telephone	Yes/No	
Newsletter	Yes/No	
Raffle Tickets	Yes/No	
Christmas Card	Yes/No	
Annual Report	Yes/No	
Contact Type (H)	Text	15

Set Contact Number as the Primary key
Save the table as Contacts

Hint: use the Lookup Wizard to
create a list of valid Contact Types
eg Individual Donor, VIP, Company,
Trust etc

CREATING OTHER TABLES

Now you can create the other tables you need using the procedures outlined above. The steps you need to follow are the same as for the Contacts table, so below you will find a list of suggested fields, their data types and field sizes together with an indication of anything different from what you have encountered already.

Table 3 Appeals table – suggested Field Names, Data Types and Field Sizes

Appeals table

Field Name	Data Type	Field Size/Format
Appeal Code	Text	10
Appeal Description	Text	50
Start Date	Date/Time	Medium Date
End Date	Date/Time	Medium Date
Appeal Cost	Currency	Currency
Appeal Target	Currency	Currency
Number Mailed	Number	Integer
Number of Responses	Number	Integer
Donations To-Date	Currency	Currency

Set Appeal Code as the Primary key
Save the table as Appeals

Figure 12 The complete Appeals table design should look like this

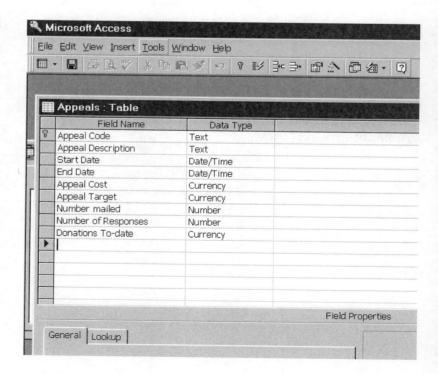

Table 4 Gifts table – suggested Field Names, Data Types and Field Sizes and hints on using Lookup Wizard

Hint: use the Lookup Wizard (in the Data Type column) to create a list of the Appeal Codes from the Appeals table. This will enable you to pick from a valid list of Appeal Codes instead of having to type in the Appeal Code on every Gift record.

Gifts table

Field Name	Data Type	Field Size/Format
Contact Number	Number	Long Integer
Date	Date/Time	Medium Date
Amount	Currency	Currency
Receipt Y/N	Yes/No	Yes/No
Appeal Code **H**	Text	10

When you click the Lookup Wizard, the operations you carry out here will be slightly different from those you used for Contact Type in the Contacts table because there you were telling the system what values to choose from eg High Value Donor, School, Trust etc. In this case you are telling the system to look up the values to choose from in another table ie the Appeals table:

- After clicking **Lookup Wizard**, you are asked how you want your lookup column to get its values.
  Leave the default as 'I want the lookup column to look up the values in a table or query'.
- Click **Next**.
  You are then asked which table or query should provide the values for your lookup column.
- Highlight **Appeals** and click **Next**.
  The next question asks which fields contain the values you want included in your lookup column.
- From the Available Fields list select **Appeal Code** and click **>** which will move it to the Selected Fields list.
- Click **Next**.
  The next question asks how wide you would like the columns in your lookup column.
- Leave the default (unless you have very long Appeal names, in which case you would put the cursor on the right-hand edge of the box containing the words 'Appeal Code' and drag it to the right) and click **Next**.
  The next question asks what label you would like for your lookup column.
- Leave the default of Appeal Code and click **Finish**.
  You are then told that the table must be saved before the relationships can be created.
- Save now? Click **Yes**.
- In the Save As window enter the name Gifts and click **OK**.
  You are then told that there is no Primary key.
- Click **Yes**.
  This will insert a Primary key for you called ID.
- Click **Save**.

Table 5 Communication Log table – suggested Field Names, Data Types and Field Sizes

Communication Log table

Field Name	Data Type	Field Size/Format
Contact Number	Number	Long Integer
Date	Date/Time	Medium Date
Communication Type (H)	Text	20
Note/Comment	Text	50

Save the table as Communication Log
You are then told that there is no Primary key. Click **Yes**
Click **Save**

Hint: use the Lookup Wizard to create a list of valid Communication Types eg Telephone Call In, Letter Out, Meeting, Dinner etc

Table 6 Notes table – suggested Field Names, Data Types and Field Sizes

Notes table

Field Name	Data Type	Field Size/Format
Contact Number	Number	Long Integer
Date	Date/Time	Medium Date
Subject (H)	Text	20
Note/Comment	Text	50

Save the table as Notes
You are then told that there is no Primary key. Click **Yes**
Click **Save**

Hint: use the Lookup Wizard to create a list of valid note Subjects eg Personal, Applications, Sponsorship etc

Now all the tables we need have been created and you should be able to see five tables on the Tables tab of the Database window. Now we need to link them together.

Linking the tables together

We shall now link the tables together as shown in the data modelling diagram (see Figure 10, page 72).

The Contacts table is our central table and we need link to it the Gifts, Communication Log and Notes tables. Then, when we select a specific contact, the system can show us only the gifts, communications and notes relevant to that contact. Similarly, we need to link the Gifts table to the Appeals table so that, by selecting a specific appeal, we can see the gifts received in response to that appeal.

TELLING THE SYSTEM WHICH TABLES TO LINK

First, you have to tell the system which tables you want to link together. Access calls these links 'relationships'.

1 With the Tables tab of the Database window showing, click the **Relationships** icon. (It is near the right-hand end of the Task bar and shows three boxes joined together.)
Note that Relationships is also on the Tools menu.

2 You should then get a Relationships window with a Show Table window overlayed on top of it.
If you don't get a Show Table window, click the **Relationships** menu item and click **Show Table**.

Note: If you followed the Lookup Wizard instructions when creating the Gifts table, then Appeals and Gifts will already be displayed. In this case just add Contacts, Communication Log and Notes.

3 The Show Table window lists the five tables in your database. One at a time, click a table name and click **Add**. **N**
All the tables will appear in the Relationships window.

4 Click **Close**.

DEFINING THE LINKS BETWEEN THE TABLES

Second, you must define the links you need between the tables. Start by creating the one to many link between the Appeals table and the Gifts table.

The field that links these two tables is the Appeal Code. You will see a line joining the Appeals table to the Gifts table already. Access created this link when you were using the Lookup Wizard so that the Appeal Code on the Gifts record would show you which Appeal Codes had already been defined on the Appeals table. You need to change this link so that the relationships between records in our database are always consistent. For example, you do not want to be able to delete an Appeals record and still have Gift records pointing to a non-existent Appeals record. To change the link you need to Edit the relationship:

1 Click on the line joining the two tables (the line will become bold) and click the **Relationships** menu item.

2 Click **Edit Relationship**.

3 Click on the words **'Enforce Referential Integrity'**.
This ensures that you always enter valid values into Appeal Code when creating new Gift records.

4 Click on the words **'Cascade Update Related Fields'**.

If, for example, you were to change an Appeal Code in the Appeals table at a later date then this changes all other references to that Appeal Code in other tables – not a good idea – don't do it!

5 Click on the words **'Cascade Delete Related Records'**.
If, for example, you were to delete an Appeal from the Appeals table then this would automatically delete that Appeal's records on related tables, in this case the Gifts table.

6 Click the **Join Type** button.
A Join Properties window appears.

7 Click on the number **3** and click **OK**.

8 Click **OK**.

You will now be back to the main Relationships window where you should be able to see that the line joining the Appeals table and the Gifts table has changed slightly. There should be a '1' above the line near to the Appeals table and a '∝' (infinity) sign above the line near to the Gifts table.

CREATING THE LINK BETWEEN TABLES

Now create the link between the Contacts and the Gifts table as follows:

1 Click on **Contact Number** in the Contacts table and drag it on top of Contact Number in the Gifts table.

2 When you release the left mouse button a small Relationship window pops up. This shows you the field you have selected (you can select more than one field but we are keeping it simple and in this case we don't need to).

3 Click on the words **'Enforce Referential Integrity'**.

4 Click on the words **'Cascade Update Related Fields'**.

5 Click on the words **'Cascade Delete Related Records'**.

6 Click the **Join Type** button.
A Join Properties window appears.

7 Click on the number **3** and click **OK**.

8 Click the **Create** button.

Repeat the above procedure to link Contacts with Communication Log by simply replacing the Gifts table by Communication Log table in the instructions above.

Repeat again, but this time replace Gifts by Notes.

Now drag each table around the Relationships window by picking up the tables (one at a time) anywhere in the Table name at the top of each table, and dragging them around the screen until the lines are all visible and not overlapping.

Figure 13 Your Relationships window should end up looking something like this

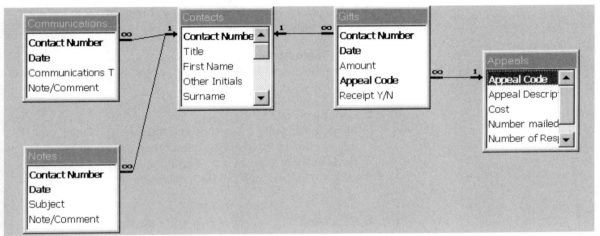

Click the **Save** icon and **close** the Relationships window.

You now have everything you need in order to start entering data. To do this you click any of the tables in the Database window and click **Open** (or double click the table name). You will then see the table laid out in spreadsheet form; this is called a Datasheet View. You can enter records directly into this, but it is not very clear. We need our tables in order to use our database (see Chapter 7), but the key to easy recording and viewing of data in Access is to design suitable forms. We will use the Forms function and create something a bit more useful because we can combine details from several tables on a single form and we can link forms together.

Setting up Access forms for entering and viewing data

Access forms have the look and feel of Windows rather than a spreadsheet. You can alter colours and fonts and you can position fields anywhere on the form instead of having them in a long line. They are more flexible because you can add function buttons and subforms to them. They are certainly nicer than tables to look at and to use when searching for and viewing individual records.

DESIGNING A FORM FOR APPEALS

Firstly, let's create a very simple form for entering details of appeals.

1 Click the **Forms** tab in the Database window and you will see two entries describing different ways to create a Form.

2 Double click on the item **Create Form by using Wizard**. The Form Wizard window appears.

3 In the Tables/Queries box, click the **down arrow** to get a list of your tables.

4 Click **Table:Appeals**. All the fields in the Appeals table appear in the Available Fields box.

5 Click the **>>**. All the fields will jump across into the Selected Fields box. (If you wanted to leave any fields out then you could select the fields you want one at a time with the '>' sign. Alternatively, click the **>>** and then put back fields you don't want with the '<' sign.)

6 Click **Next**. You are asked what layout you want for your form. (If you click each one in turn you will be shown an idea of what it will look like.)

7 Click **Columnar** and click **Next**. You are asked what style you would like.

8 Click each style in turn to see which one you like best. Highlight your preference and click **Next**. You are then asked for a title for the form.

9 Leave the form title defaulted to Appeals. You are also asked if you want to open the form or modify the form's design. Leave it set to 'Open the form to view or enter information'.

10 Click **Finish**. Your form for entering details of appeals will appear, and Appeals will appear in the Forms tab.

11 Close the Form.

Entering appeal details

You can enter appeal details now or at any future time as follows:

- Click **Forms**, click **Appeals** and click **Open**.

- Move between different Appeal records using the buttons at the bottom of the screen:

  - for 'go to the first record in the table' press **I◀**;
  - for 'go to the previous record' press **◀**;
  - for 'go to the next record' press **▶**;
  - for 'go to the last record' press **▶I**;
  - for 'clear the screen ready to enter a new record' press **▶ ✳**.

  Note that at this point these buttons will have no effect because we have not yet entered any data.

To search for a particular record you can also use the Find function which is on the Edit menu.

Figure 14 A sample Appeals form

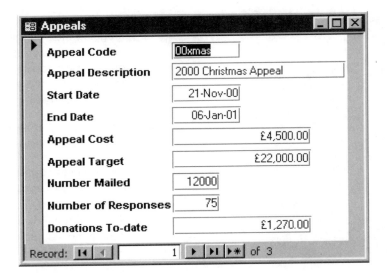

DESIGNING A FORM FOR CONTACTS

Next we will create a form for the basic contact details. Follow the instructions above, but for 'Appeals' read 'Contacts'. This will give you a nice-looking form to enter contact details into, to modify details of existing contacts and to find contacts easily at a later date. If you didn't add too many extra fields when you created the Contacts table, you could also fit the gifts onto this form. Leave any blank space you have so you can add fields to the table later. Besides, you will need a small amount of space for a little trick that comes later.

MODIFYING THE LAYOUT OF A FORM

At any time you can re-design the form and, in particular, move items around on the form. This applies to any form you create but as you have just created a Contacts form then experiment with this one.

1 From the Forms tab in the Database window, click **Contacts** and click the **Design** button. What appears is the form you created with a grid of lines across it and with each field name appearing twice. Needless to say, the first occurrence is the Field Name as it appears on the screen and the second occurrence is where the data will be entered.

2 Put the cursor in any of these fields and drag them to any position on the form. The two names move together as you drag, thus keeping the description with the field itself. The grid lines are there to help you line things up.

3 You can make the whole form larger (or smaller) by re-sizing the Form window itself. You do this by:

- dragging the right-hand edge of the form to make the form wider (or narrower);
- dragging the top line (not the bottom line) of the grey bar at the bottom of the window (with the words Form Footer in it) to make the form longer (or shorter).

4 You can alter the size of each data item's description or the size of the space where the data will be entered by:

- clicking in the description or the field. Small box shapes called handles appear around the description or field you selected;
- the top left handle is larger than the others. Dragging this handle moves just the selected description or field. In this way you can move the field separately from its description. This is useful for lining up data entry fields whose descriptions are different lengths, see example form below (Figure 15);
- Dragging the other handles makes the description or field longer, shorter, thicker or thinner.

5 When you have finished modifying the Form layout, Close the Form. You will be asked if you want to save changes. Click **Yes**.

Figure 15 A sample Contacts form (the two buttons on the right-hand side are explained later under the section 'Making it easier to navigate the database', page 90)

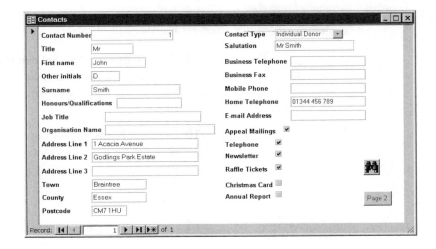

DESIGNING A FORM FOR CONTACT GIFTS, COMMUNICATIONS AND NOTES

We will now create a single form that contains the basic details of the contact (just enough to provide an exact identification), plus details of all their gifts, all their communications and all the notes we have made about them.

What we will do is create a form with two tabs. The first tab will show the gifts and communications and the second will show the notes. Take the following steps to design your form:

1 From the Forms tab in the Database window click **Create Form by using Wizard**.

2 In the Tables/Queries box, click the **down arrow** to get a list of your tables.

3 Click **Table:Contacts**.

4 One at a time, select the fields you want on the form eg **Contact Number**, **Surname**, **Job Title**, **Organisation**, by highlighting the Field Name and clicking **>**.

5 Click **Next**.
You are asked what layout you want for your form.

6 Click **Justified** and click **Next**.
You are asked what style you would like.

7 Highlight your preference and click **Next**.
You are then asked for title for the form.

8 Overwrite the default with a descriptive name like 'Contact Gifts, Communications and Notes'.

You are also asked if you want to open the form or modify the form's design.

9 Click on **Modify The Form's Design** and click **Finish**.
The form appears with your selected fields strung across the form and a set of grid lines over the form, ie you are in design mode.

10 Drag the **Form Footer** (using the top line of the footer bar) down to the bottom of the window to give you space to enter the details of gifts, communications and notes. The Form Footer is immediately underneath the second line of data fields.

11 Click the **Tab Control** button on the new tool bar that has probably appeared at the top of the screen.
(If this tool bar did not appear, then click **View** on the Menu bar and then click **Toolbox** from the dropdown menu.)

12 Move the cursor to a point near the left-hand side of the form and just under the last line of Contact table fields. Depress the left mouse button and drag to the bottom of the form (just above the footer) and across to the right to a point about one and a half grid lines in from the right-hand corner. Then release the button.
A box appears with two tabs in it and you have a gap down the right-hand side of the form. The tabs will have the names Tab01 and Tab02 (or two other consecutive numbers) or possibly Page01 and Page02 (or two other consecutive numbers).

13 Click the **Properties** icon on the Task bar (it looks like a hand holding a piece of paper or a box with a small box on the top right-hand corner).
A Page window appears. It has five tabs: Format, Data, Event, Other, All. It should be on Other and the Name should be highlighted.

14 Overtype the Name (Page01) with 'Gifts and Communications' and hit Enter.

15 Click the other tab on the form and in the Page window highlight Page02 and overtype it with Notes and hit Enter.

16 Close the Page window.
Don't bother with any of the other tabs of the Page window.

If you followed the above, the Notes tab on the form should be selected. If it isn't then click the Notes tab. To put the Notes on this tab we are now going to insert a subform:

17 Click the **Subform/Subreport** button from the Toolbox tool bar (again you might need to select **View** from the Menu bar and then select **Toolbox** to display the tool bar).
As you move the mouse back across the Notes tab of your form, a block will be highlighted showing you where you can position the subform.

18 Drag the mouse from the top left corner of the highlighted block to the bottom right corner of the block.
When you release the mouse button the Subform/Subreport Wizard appears. You are asked if you want to use an existing form or build a new one from tables and queries.

19 Leave it set to Use existing Tables and Queries and click **Next**. A familiar selection screen appears.

20 Select **Notes** from the Tables and Queries list. Select all fields except ID and Contact Number and click **Next**. You are then asked to define which fields link your main form to this sub-form.

21 Because of the relationships we set up earlier, the system knows that Notes is linked to Contacts by the Contact Number so leave 'Choose From a List' selected and leave 'Show Notes for each record in Contacts using Contact Number' highlighted and click **Next**.
You are then asked to name your subform.

22 Leave it defaulted to Notes subform and click **Finish**.

23 The Notes subform now appears on your Notes tab.

24 Click the **Gifts and Communications** tab.

25 Repeat actions 18 to 23 above replacing 'Notes' by 'Gifts'. After action 23 when the Gifts subform appears, drag the bottom of the subform to about halfway down the area of the Gifts and Communications tab.

26 Repeat actions 18 to 23 above replacing 'Notes' by 'Communication Log', but in action 19, start the top left corner just below the highlighted Gifts subform. After action 23 when the Communication Log subform appears drag the bottom of the subform to the bottom of the Gifts and Communications tab.

27 Click the **Save** icon and **Close** the form.

Suggestion: maximise the area of the subform by dragging the little square in the middle at the bottom of the subform down to the bottom of the Notes tab area.

Figure 16 A sample form for
Contact Gifts, Communications
and Notes (the button on the
right-hand side is explained later
under the section 'Making it easier to navigate the database',
below)

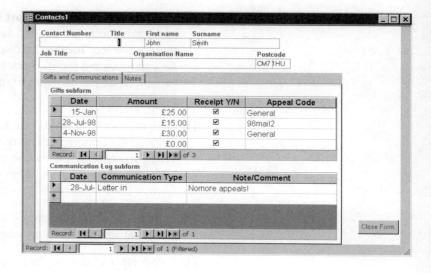

Having got to this point you now have three (or four if you created the separate Gifts tab) forms that you can open from the
Forms tab in the Database window and start to use.

Making it easier to navigate the database

One of the things that makes a database easy or difficult to use is
the way in which you find your way around the system. This database will be easier to use if you can link two forms together
(particularly your Contacts form and your Contact Gifts,
Communications and Notes form). It will also be easier to use if
you have a shortcut method of reaching your database from your
Windows desktop and if you have a menu or 'switchboard' which
appears automatically when you enter the database. We will create
those things now.

LINKING TWO FORMS TOGETHER

When looking at the details of a contact as defined in the
Contacts table it would be helpful to be able to see the gifts, communication and notes associated with that contact with a single
mouse click. This can be done by introducing a Command Button
into the Contacts form and another to the Contact Gifts,
Communications and Notes which will enable you to move from
one form to the other.

1 From the Forms tab in the Database window, select **Contacts**
and click **Design**.

2 From the Toolbox tool bar, click the **Command Button** icon.

3 Move the cursor over the form and drag to create a small box in the right-hand corner (or other suitable blank space). The Command Button Wizard appears with two lists, Categories and Actions.

4 Select **Form Operations** from the Categories list and select **Open Form** from the Actions list.

5 Click **Next**.
You then get a list of forms displayed.

6 Click **Contact Gifts, Communications and Notes**.

7 Click **Next**.
You are then asked if you want the button to find specific information.

8 Click on the words **'Open the form and find specific data to display'**.

9 Click **Next**.
You are then asked which fields contain matching data.

10 Click **Contact Number** on both lists and click **Next**.
You are then asked if you want text or a picture on the button.

11 Click on the word **'Text'**, replace the words 'Open Form' with 'Page 2'. **W**

12 Click **Next**.
You are then asked to name the button.

13 Leave the name defaulted to Command01 (or any other number that Access displays) and click **Finish**.

14 Re-size the button if you wish using the handles.

15 For convenience, you could also put a Find button on the form itself:

- select and position a **Command Button** as described in the second and third bullet points above;
- select **Record Navigation** from the Categories list and **Find Record** from the Actions list;
- click **Next**;
- when asked for Text or Picture on the button, leave it defaulted to a Picture of Binoculars2;
- click **Next**;
- leave the button name defaulted to Command02 (or other number) and click **Finish**;
- re-size the button if you wish.

Warning: If when you have finished adding Command buttons to this form, you Open the Form to see how it looks in real life, you will get a Syntax Error if you click on the Page 2 button. This will occur until you have entered data for at least one contact.

16 Click the **Save** icon and **close** the form.

17 From the Forms tab in the Database window, select **Contact Gifts, Communications and Notes** and click **Design**.

18 From the Toolbox tool bar, click the **Command Button** icon.

19 Move the cursor over the form and drag to create a small box in the right-hand corner (or other suitable blank space). **W** The Command Button Wizard appears with two lists, Categories and Actions.

20 Select **Form Operations** from the Categories list and **Close Form** from the Actions list.

21 Click **Next**.
You are then asked what you want on the button.

22 Click on the word 'Text', leave the words as 'Close Form' and click **Next**.
You are then asked to name the button.

23 Leave the button name defaulted to Command03 (or any other number) and click **Finish**.

24 Click the **Save** icon and **close** the form. **W**

Warning: You may first need to drag the right hand edge of the grid line area further to the right to make more space.

Warning: if you add a Page 1 button to the Contact Gifts, Communications and Notes form in the same way as you add the Page 2 button to the Contacts form, then you create a circular relationship and you will never be able to find a different contact.

Your two forms are now linked. Check the operation by opening the Contacts form on the Forms tab of the Database window and clicking the Page 2 button, see that it swaps to the other form and click the Close Form button to see that it swaps back again. (See earlier warning about entering data. Also, you won't be able to check the operation of the Find button until you have entered several records.)

CREATING A SWITCHBOARD (MENU)

A menu gives quick access to your forms and has an exit function to close down the database. We will put the menu over the top of the Database window. You can then easily click to this Database window if you want to add any functionality to your database or create special reports at a later date.

1 From the Tools menu highlight **Database Utilities** and click **Switchboard Manager**.
You will probably get a message saying that it was unable to find a valid switchboard and asking if would you like to create one.

2 Click **Yes**.
The Switchboard Manager window will appear.

3 Click **New**.

4 In the Switchboard Page Name enter the name you want for your database.
You will probably put your organisation's name followed by Contacts Database.

5 Click **OK**.

6 Highlight the name you entered above and click **Edit**.
You will then see your database's name and an 'Items in this Switchboard' box which is empty.

7 Click **New**.
The Edit Switchboard Item Window appears.

8 In the Text field enter something like 'General Contact Information'.

9 From the Command list select **Open Form in Edit Mode**.

10 From the Form list select **Contacts**.

11 Click **OK**.

12 Click **New** again.

13 In the Text field enter 'Gifts, Communications and Notes'.

14 From the Command list select **Open Form in Edit Mode**.

15 From the Form list select **Gifts, Communications and Notes**.

16 Click **OK**.

17 If you created a separate Gifts form then:

- click **New** again;
- in the Text field enter 'All Gifts';
- from the Command list select **Open Form in Edit Mode**;
- from the Form list select **Gifts** and click **OK**.

18 Click **New** again.

19 In the Text field enter Appeal Information.

20 From the Command list select **Open Form in Edit Mode**.

21 From the Form list select **Appeals** and click **OK**.

22 Click **New** again.

23 In the Text field enter Exit Database.

24 From the Command list select **Exit Application** and click **OK**.

25 Click **Close**.

26 Ensure that the switchboard name that you entered earlier is highlighted and click **Make Default**.

27 Click **Close**.

You will now find that a table called Switchboard Items has appeared in your Database Tables window and also a new form called Switchboard has appeared in your Database Forms window. Now what you need to do is make the menu come up every time you open the database. You do this by the following:

- Click the **Tools** menu item and click **Startup**.

- Select **Switchboard** from the Display Form/Page list (leave all the other things as they are for now) and click **OK**.

From now on, every time you open your database you will get the menu displayed. **Close** the database, ie exit from Access, then open up the database again to prove that it works.

Figure 17 A sample switchboard or menu

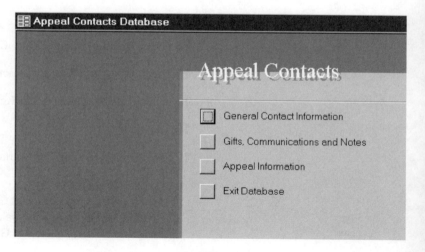

CREATING A SHORTCUT ON THE DESKTOP

In order to enter the database quickly it is helpful to have a shortcut to it on the desktop. One easy way to create a shortcut is:

1 From the desktop click the **Start** button.

2 Highlight **Find** and click **Files and Folders**.
A Find:All Files window appears.

3 In the Named field type in ***.mdb** and click **Find Now**.
The system will display a list of all the Access databases on the disk (it should be a very short list).

4 Position the cursor over the name of your database and right click the mouse.

5 From the displayed list click **Create Shortcut**.
You will get a message 'Windows cannot create a shortcut here. Do you want the shortcut to be placed on the desktop instead?'

6 Click **Yes**.

7 Close the Find Files window and you will see the shortcut has appeared on the desktop.

8 If you don't like the name:

- right click on the shortcut icon;
- click **Rename** from the list;
- type the new name;
- click in a blank space on the desktop.

Double clicking this shortcut will open Access, open your database and display your menu.

Recording and viewing information about your supporters

You can now enter data about your supporters and your appeals into any of the forms (and subforms).

ENTERING APPEAL INFORMATION

Before you can enter gift items against the relevant appeal, you need to set up your appeal records:

1 Click the **Appeals Information** button on the switchboard.
We will first set up an Appeal called 'General' to cope with any gifts received that are not in response to a particular appeal or campaign.

2 Enter 'General' into the Appeal code of the first Appeal record and leave all the other fields empty.

3 Tab through all the fields on the form or click the ▶ ✳ symbol to get to the end of the file ready to enter another record.

4 Set up all other current Appeal records, clicking the ▶ ✳ to set up the next record each time.

5 Close the Appeal Form.

ENTERING CONTACT INFORMATION

Next, set up all your contacts:

1 Click the **General Contact Information** button on the switchboard.
First we will set up an anonymous donor record.

2 Into the first record enter 'Anonymous' into the Surname and leave all the other fields empty.
There is an advantage in setting up the anonymous donor record first: it will be record number 1, so if you use the Gifts form to enter gifts you simply enter '1' into the Contact Number for every anonymous gift you get from individuals, corporates or any other source.

3 Set up all your contact records, clicking the ▶ ✳ to set up the next record each time.

IMPORTING NAMES AND ADDRESSES FROM OLD SYSTEMS

Names and addresses (and other fields that correspond to other fields in your Contacts table eg telephone number) can be imported to Access as long as they are in one of a number of standard formats. These formats include text files (CSV and TXT), Microsoft Access, Microsoft Excel and dBase. **N**

You import a file as follows:

1 When in the main Database window, select the **File** menu, highlight **Get External Data**, click **Import**.
An Import window appears that is the same as a normal Open Files window.

2 From the Files of Type drop down list, highlight the type of file that contains your names and addresses, then find your file, highlight it and click **Import**.
(If you choose a text file then you will now have to tell the system how the file is delimited, ie what character separates each field. This is usually a comma.)

Note: ensure that the first record contains column headings, for instance the first row of an Excel spreadsheet. In order to make this import function work, you must ensure that the column headings in the file to be imported are exactly the same as the names of the fields the data will be imported into in the Contacts table eg Title, First Name, Surname, Organisation Name, Address Line 1 etc.

3 If you choose an **Excel** file (or when you have specified the delimiting character for text files), the next screen shows a sample of your data. Click the box to indicate that the **First row contains column headings**. Assuming the data looks OK then click **Next**.
You are then asked where you would like to store your data.

4 Click **In an existing table**, click the **drop down list**, highlight **Contacts**, click **Next** and when the next screen comes up, click **Finish**.

5 You get a message when the import is finished.

6 Click **OK** and you are returned to the main Access screen.

7 Open the Contacts table and scroll the records to see the names and addresses you have imported.

FINDING CONTACT RECORDS

Your normal everyday searching will be from the main Contacts form, the one you put the Find button on, which is the first item on your switchboard.

1 Open the **Contacts** form and it will come up with the first record on the file which should be the anonymous donor.

2 Put the cursor into the field that you want to search on, eg Surname.

3 Click your **Find** button.
The Find and Replace window appears.

4 Type what you want to find in the **Find What** field and click the **Find Next** button.
If there are many items matching your criteria, eg the Surname Smith, then clicking **Find Next** retrieves the records one at a time.

Note that there are some particularly useful features of the Find function. One is the Match field, where the options are: Any Part of Field, Whole Field and Start of Field. The second is the Look In Field, which contains an entry that is the name of the form. If you select this, the Find function will search every field defined on the form in the entire database. This can take a long time in a big database but it can be useful for things like searching for part of an address when you don't know which line the information is in.

You can search on any field in the database. The same Find function works in the same way on any form in the database by using the Find icon on the Task bar.

Chapter summary

You have now created an Access database and recorded details of your Appeal programmes and details of all your contacts. You are now in a position to start using the database by recording the communications you have with your contacts, preparing mailshots and recording income.

CHAPTER 7

Using a more advanced fundraising database

This chapter gives very detailed step by step instructions of how to use the Access database you created in Chapter 6. We will discuss how to record communications with people, how to mail people, how to record income, and how to report on and analyse the income from your campaigns.

Recording communications with contacts

You can use your forms to note the dates you speak to contacts in your database, when you send them a letter or other communication and to briefly note the contents. This will prove invaluable for campaigns which do not involve mass mailing eg corporate fundraising, trust fundraising and big-gift fundraising. To do this:

1 Go into your database.

2 Select the first item on the switchboard and find the contact you require.

3 Click the **Page 2** button and enter the details in the appropriate subform.
Each subform works in the same way as the main forms. If, for example, you enter data into the Notes subform, you will notice that the system automatically enters this into the item it creates in the Notes table.

4 Click the **Close Form** button to return to the main Contact Form when you have finished and want to find another contact.

5 You can of course select the second item on the menu and remain completely within the Contact Gifts, Communications and Notes form (Page 2) if the contact details on this page are enough to find your desired contacts eg Name and Postcode. However, it is probably better to always come from the main Contacts screen where you can see more general details of the contact before looking at their gifts, communications and notes.

Mailing

MAILING EVERYONE ON THE DATABASE

You do not need to have your database open to do this:

1 Open **Word**.
You will probably have a template for letters, so open that.

2 Type your letter:

- leave name and address blank;
- start with the date;
- type salutation 'Dear' followed by a blank;
- type your letter.

3 Click **Tools** and then click **Mail Merge**.
The Mail Merge Helper pops up. The first item is Main Document with a Create button under it.

4 Click the **Create** button.
You get a choice of Form Letters, Mailing Labels, Envelopes and Catalog.

5 Click **Form Letters**.
You get a choice of Active Window or New Main Document.

6 Click **Active Window**.
The system fills in the Merge Type you have selected and the name of the document below the Create button and gives you a new button called Edit.

7 Under Data Source there is a **Get Data** button. Click this button.
You get a choice of Create Data Source, Open Data Source, Use Address Book and Header Options.

8 Click **Open Data Source**.
An Open Data Source window appears which is a normal Open Files window.

9 From the Files Of Type list select **MS Access Databases**.
You then get a list of all Access databases in your default directory (usually My Documents).

10 Highlight your database and click **Open**.
A small Microsoft Access window appears with two tabs, Tables and Queries.

11 Highlight **Contacts** on the Tables tab and click **OK**.
After a few seconds you get the message that 'Word found no merge fields in your main document'. Don't worry about it, we will set them up now.

12 Click the **Edit Main Document** button.
You will now see that two new items have appeared on a Task bar, Insert Merge Field and Insert Word Field.

13 Position your cursor to where you want your name and address to be entered and click **Insert Merge Field**.
This gives you a list of all the fields in your Contacts Table.

14 Click **Title** and <<Title>> pops into your document.

15 Type a space (or the First Name will be immediately next to the Title), click **Insert Merge Field** and click **First Name**.

16 Carry on through all the fields that you need eg space, Insert Merge Field, Surname, Insert Merge Field, Honours/Qualifications, Enter (or however you start a new line), Insert Merge Field, Job Title, Enter, Insert Merge Field, Organisation Name, Enter, Insert Merge Field, Address Line 1, Enter etc for the rest of the address.

17 Position the cursor to one space beyond the salutation 'Dear', click **Insert Merge Field** and click **Salutation**.

18 When you have inserted all the Merge fields you need into your letter you have to go back to the Mail Merge Helper. To do this you can either:

   – click **Tools** and then **Mail Merge** or
   – click on the **Mail Merge Helper** icon you now find on the same line as the Insert Merge Field button.

19 Go to Merge Data With The Document.
This has two buttons: Merge and Query Options. If you click **Query Options** you can see that it can Filter (ie select) Records and Sort Records. It can filter and sort on any of the allowable Merge fields (not just those you selected to put into the letter). We will use this later.

20 Click **Cancel** to return to the Mail Merge Helper.
Under the Merge button you will see the default options that it sets ie Suppress Blank Lines in Addresses and Merge to new document.

21 Click **Merge**.
You get the Merge box displayed. The Merge To field is set to New Document. You also get another chance to set the Query Options.

22 Click the **Merge** button.
In a few seconds the first of your mail-merged letters appears on the screen.

23 You can then check, alter, print and save your letters if you wish.

24 Click **Window** on the Menu bar and click **Document 1** (assuming this is your Form Letter) to switch to your form letter and save it.
You can use this letter again in the future, suitably amended, for another mail merge.

The operation is now complete. If you look at the bottom of your screen, you might find that you have ended up with one or more copies of the Contacts database opened and not closed by the Mail Merge function. If so, just click on each one in turn and close it.

MAILING A SELECTED GROUP OR SUB-SET OF CONTACTS ON THE DATABASE

Unlike in Chapter 4 where we said that using the Filter Records function within the Query Options function of Mail Merge was of little value, this time it is of immense value. The reason for this is that you can use any of the fields in the Contacts table in the query statements. Consequently you can, for example, select on different values of Contact Type. If you wanted to send a standard letter to all the people on your database who had the Category of 'VIP' then you would follow the instructions above under 'Mailing everyone on the database' up to point 19. You then:

1 Click **Query Options**.
You get Filter Records and Sort Records tabs.

2 Scroll down the Field box on the Filter Records tab and highlight **Contact Type**.
The Comparison field defaults to Equal To.

3 Type **VIP** in the Compare To box and click **OK**.

4 Click **Merge**.
The Merge window is displayed.

5 Click **Merge**.
Word will produce your letters just for VIPs.

Before you selected the Contacts table as your Data Source in Mail Merge above there were two options: Tables or Queries. Selecting Queries is another way to select a sub-set from the database to mail. You haven't created any Queries yet but this will come soon when you enter some income and want to send thank you letters only to those people who sent you money today.

Recording income

This is very easy and follows the same pattern of entering data as for communications and notes which was discussed at the beginning of this chapter:

1 Open your database.

2 Select the first item on the switchboard.
This should be the General Contact Information item which will bring up your main Contacts form.

3 Find the contact you require.

4 Click the **Page 2** button.

5 Enter the gift details into the Gifts subform.

6 If you have several cheques, then click **Close Form** (which will return you to your main Contacts form), find the next contact, click Page 2 etc.

If you are in the habit of sending out donation forms on which is printed the Contact Number then you will have created a separate Gifts form plus a Multiple Gifts Entry item on the switchboard. If you work like this, then open the Gifts form and enter the gift details this way. (You won't get a visual check that you have entered the gift against the correct contact, but the system will ensure that you enter it against a valid Contact Number.)

Sending thank you letters

Having entered all the gifts you have received in one day, you can select from the database the relevant supporters to send thank you letters. You do this by creating an Access Query.

In the Query you define conditions that will select only those supporters whose gifts you have received on the relevant day. You also define what data items you want from the records of these contacts, for instance the gift details and the donors' names and addresses. You then use this Query as the Data Source for a Word mail merge. Needless to say, we can also include the value of the gift in the text of every letter.

Two ways of using Query will be described, although you only need the first (and easier) one for this exercise. The second is included to introduce you to the full functions of Query. You may want to use these at a later date for more complex selections when you are researching and analysing your database.

EASY QUERY, MORE COMPLEX MAIL MERGE

1 Open your database and click the **Queries** tab in the Database window.
If you can't see any part of the Database window, ie because it is completely hidden behind the switchboard, then click the Window menu item and click the item near the bottom which says your database name followed by :Database.

2 The Queries box will contain two entries describing the different ways of creating Queries.

3 Double click **Create Query by using Wizard**. The Simple Query Wizard appears and you are asked what fields you want in your query.

4 From the Tables/Queries list, select **Tables: Contacts**.

5 From the Available Fields select **Title** through to **Postcode**.
As the name and address fields are one after the other in the table then after highlighting **Title** and clicking **>** you can just continue to click **>** until all the fields down to and including Postcode have been selected. Don't select any other fields nor use the **>>** to select all the fields because you don't need them.

6 Now go back to the Tables/Queries list and select **Tables: Gifts**.

7 From the Available Fields select **Date**, **Amount**, **Appeal Code** and **Receipt Y/N**.

8 Click **Next**.

9 Leave the next screen defaulted to 'Detail (show every field of every record)' and click **Next**.
You are asked 'What title do you want for your query?'

10 Type in **'All Gifts'**.
You are also asked 'Do you want to open the query or modify the query design?'

11 Leave it defaulted to 'Open the query to view information' and click **Finish**.
You will then see the result of running the query (as a window called All Gifts: Select Query) displayed in datasheet format.

12 Check the datasheet and check you have all the fields that you expected.

13 **Close** the datasheet.
You will see that All Gifts has appeared in the Queries box.

14 The Query is complete and you can **close** the database.

15 Enter Word and create your standard thank you letter.

Proceed with a mail merge as described above under 'Mailing everyone on the database' (see page 100) except that:

1 When you get to the Data Source section choose **Queries** (instead of Tables) and select **All Gifts**.

2 Insert all the merge fields including the Amount field in the body of your letter, eg Thank you for your gift of <<Amount>>. Note that this will automatically put a '£' sign in because the field is described in Access as a currency field.

3 When you get to the Merge data with the Document section choose **Query Options** before doing the Merge.

4 On the Filter Records tab, from the Field list select **Surname**, from the Comparison list select **Not Equal To** and in the Compare To box enter '**Anonymous**'.
(Otherwise you will produce thank you letters for anonymous donations).

5 In the Field box under Surname select **Date** (leave the And/Or box set to And), leave the Comparison defaulted to **Equal To** and in the Compare To box enter **today's date** (in any normal format eg dd/mm/yy).

6 Click **OK**.

7 Click **Merge**.
The Merge window is displayed.

8 Click **Merge**.
Word will produce today's thank you letters.

MORE COMPLEX QUERY, EASY MAIL MERGE

1 Open your database and click the **Queries** tab in the Database window.

2 Double click **Create Query in Design View**.
A Show Table window appears with three tabs: Tables, Queries and Both.

3 From the Tables tab, highlight **Contacts** and click **Add**, highlight **Gifts** and click **Add**.

4 Click **Close**.
You get a window called Query 1: Select Query which shows the two tables you selected.

It also shows the one to many relationship between them, plus a table with rows labelled Field, Table, Sort, Show, Criteria and Or.

5 Enter into the Field row the field names of every field you want in your query.

You do this by dragging the fields from the tables or selecting the fields from the drop down list in each Field cell. For example:

- drag **Title** from the Contacts table into the first Field cell. Note that the corresponding Table cell is automatically filled in by the system;
- click the next Field cell.
  (Alternatively, click the drop down arrow and click Contacts:First Name);
- continue across the Field cells by selecting all the fields you need (in either of the above ways) eg Other Initials, Job Title, Organisation Name, Address Line 1 etc from the Contacts table and Date, Amount, Appeal Code and Receipt Y/N from the Gifts table.

6 Click the **Criteria** cell underneath Surname and type into it **not="Anonymous"**.

7 Hit the **Enter** key (or click the mouse in another cell).

8 In the Criteria cell underneath Date, enter an '=' sign and today's date eg **=1/4/01**.

9 Hit the **Enter** key.

10 Click the **Save** icon.
A Save As window appears.

11 Type '**Today's Thank You Letters** ' into the Query Name box and click **OK**.

12 Click the **Run** icon (!) to see that the query selects the correct records.
This shows you a datasheet view of the selected records.

13 **Close** the datasheet.
You will now see that Today's Thank You Letters has been added to the Queries list.

14 The Query is complete and you can **close** the database.

15 Open **Word** and create your standard thank you letter.

Proceed with a mail merge as described above in 'Mailing everyone on the database' (see page 100) except that:

1 When you get to the Data Source section choose **Queries** (instead of Tables) and select **Today's Thank You Letters**.

2 Insert all the merge fields including the Amount field in the body of your letter.

3 Click **Merge** and continue as before.
Note: there is no need to use Query Options.

Tomorrow and each subsequent day when you receive gifts you will have to amend the query to reflect today's date. To do this you simply:

1 Highlight **Today's Thank You Letters** on the Queries tab in the Database window and click **Design**.

2 Alter the date in the Criteria cell underneath Date to be today's date and hit **Enter**.

3 Click the **Save** icon.

4 Click the **Run** icon to see that it selects the correct records.

5 **Close** the database.

Analysing income

Having completed your mailing and received donations in response, you will want to consider which types of income analysis will be useful to you. Below we show how to create a few useful reports. The first is a 'top donors' report containing details of who has given the most money. The second shows an analysis of the gifts received each month and the third shows the gifts received for a particular appeal. Report creation can be complex. In the examples below we shall use basic reporting wizards, but if you become familiar with designing Access reports, you can produce more complex reports yourself.

TOP DONORS REPORT

This is a very easy report to produce. You should already have a Query called All Gifts. If you didn't produce it earlier go back to the section where it was described (see page 104) and create it now.

1 Click the **Reports** tab of the Database window.

2 Double click **Create Report by using Wizard**.
The Report Wizard appears.

3 From the Choose the Table or Query list select **Query: All Gifts**.

4 From Available Fields select: **Title**, **Surname**, **Organisation Name**, **Postcode**, **Amount**, **Appeal Code** and **Date**.

5 Click **Next**.
You are then asked 'How do you want to view your data?'

6 Highlight **By Gifts** and click **Next**.

7 Ignore the question 'Do you want to add any grouping levels?'

8 Click **Next**.
You are then asked 'What sort order do you want for your records?'

9 In field 1:

- select **Amount**;
- click the box which has an 'A' over a 'Z' with a downward pointing arrow beside it; it will then change to a 'Z' over an 'A' with a downward arrow, ie you have changed the order from ascending (lowest to highest) to descending (highest to lowest);
- click **Next**;

You will then be asked 'How would you like to lay out your report?'

10 Leave the Layout defaulted to Tabular and change the Orientation to **Landscape**.

11 Click **Next**.
The next question is 'What style would you like?'

12 For now leave the default and click **Next**.
You can experiment with these later.
The last question is 'What title do you want for your report?'

13 Type '**Top Donors**' in the box, leave Preview the Report defaulted and click **Finish**.
The report is displayed on the screen.

14 Click the **Print** icon on the Task bar and the whole report will be printed.

15 If you don't want to print the whole report, but for instance just the top 20 or 30 records, you can:

- click the **File** menu and click the **Print** item on this menu instead of clicking the Print icon;

– then click **Pages** and enter '**1**' in the From box and '**1**' in the To box and click **OK**.

This, surprisingly enough, will print only the first page of the report.

16 **Close** the Preview window.
Note that Top Donors has appeared on the Reports tab.

You can run this report at any time by highlighting **Top Donors** on the Reports tab and selecting **Print** from the File menu (or just clicking the **Print** icon on the Task bar if you want to print the entire report).

GIFTS THIS MONTH

This simple report will be valuable for end-of-the-month accounting purposes to show the total month's donations, and if run during the month, it will give an indication of how things are going so far. First, you will need to modify the All Gifts query to select just the gifts for this month and then you can produce the report.

1 On the Queries tab of the Database window:

– highlight **All Gifts**;
– click the **Copy** icon;
– click the **Paste** icon;
– type **Gifts This Month** into the Query Name box;
– click **OK**.

2 With **Gifts This Month** highlighted on the Queries tab, click the **Design** button.
The Select Query window appears.

3 Scroll across the table until you get to the Date field.

4 Into the **Criteria** cell under **Date**, enter a logical expression to represent this month only, eg for April 2001 you could enter **>31/03/01 and <01/05/01**.

5 Hit the **Enter** key and **close** the Select Query window.
You will then be asked if you want to save the changes to the design of the query.

6 Click **Yes**.

7 Go to the **Reports** tab and double click **Create Report by using Wizard**.

8 Select **Gifts this Month** from the Choose Table or Query list.

9 From Available Fields select: **Title, Surname, Organisation Name, Postcode, Amount, Appeal Code** and **Date**.

10 Click **Next**.
You will be asked 'How do you want to view your data?'

11 Highlight **By Gifts** and click **Next**.
You are then asked 'Do you want to add any grouping levels?'

12 Highlight **Appeal Code**, click the **>** and click **Next**.
You are then asked 'What sort order and summary information do you want for your detail records?'

13 In box 1, click the **drop down arrow** and click **Date**.

14 Click the **Summary Options** button.

15 On the Amount line click the **Sum** and **Average** boxes, under Show click **Summary Only** and click **OK**.

16 Click **Next**.
The next question is 'How would you like to lay out your report?'

17 Leave the Layout defaulted to Stepped and change the Orientation to **Landscape**.

18 Click **Next**.
The next question is 'What style would you like?'

19 Leave the default and click **Next**.
The last question is 'What title do you want for your report?'

20 Type **Gifts This Month** in the box, leave Preview the Report defaulted and click **Finish**.
The report is displayed on the screen.

21 Click the **Print** icon on the task bar and the report will be printed.

You can produce this report for any time period, from days to years, by simply altering the time period in the Query.

GIFTS THIS APPEAL

As well as knowing how you are doing this month you may also want to know how the latest appeal is progressing, irrespective of the time period. For this, you follow the same procedure as for the previous report with a few minor alterations.

1 On the Queries tab of the Database window:

- highlight **All Gifts**;
- click the **Copy** icon;
- click the **Paste** icon;
- type **Gifts for ...... Appeal** (the name of your appeal) into the Query Name box;
- click **OK**.

2 With **Gifts for .... Appeal** highlighted on the Queries tab, click the **Design** button.
Select Query window appears.

3 Scroll across the table until you get to the **Appeal Code** field.

4 Into the **Criteria** cell under **Appeal Code** enter a logical expression to represent this appeal only, eg for appeal mailing 1 you could enter **="Mailing 1"**.

5 Hit the **Enter** key and **close** the Select Query window.
You will be asked if you want to save the changes to the design of the query.

6 Click **Yes**.

7 Go to the Reports tab and double click **Create Report by using Wizard**.

8 Select **Gifts for .... Appeal** from the Choose Table or Query list.

9 From Available Fields select: **Title**, **Surname**, **Organisation Name**, **Postcode**, **Amount**, **Appeal Code** and **Date**.

10 Click **Next**.
You are then asked 'How do you want to view your data?'

11 Highlight **By Gifts** and click **Next**.
You are then asked 'Do you want to add any grouping levels?'

12 Highlight **Date**, click the **>**, click the **Grouping Options** button, select **Day** from the Grouping Intervals list and click **OK**.

13 Click **Next**.
You are then asked 'What sort order and summary information do you want for your detail records?'

14 In box 1, click the **drop down arrow** and click **Date**.

15 Click the **Summary Options** button.

16 On the Amount line click the **Sum** and **Average** boxes.

Note: if you wanted all of the detail lines you could click **Detail and Summary** instead of Summary Only above.

17 Under Show click **Summary Only** and click **OK**.

18 Click **Next**. Ⓝ
The next question is 'How would you like to lay out your report?'

19 Leave the Layout defaulted to **Stepped** and change the Orientation to **Landscape**.

20 Click **Next**.
The next question is 'What style would you like?'

21 Leave the default and click **Next**.
The last question is 'What title do you want for your report?'

22 Type **Gifts for .... Appeal** in the box, leave Preview the Report defaulted and click **Finish**.
The report is displayed on the screen.

23 Click the **Print** icon on the taskbar and the report will be printed.

The report will give you a total per day of the gifts received for the specified Appeal Code.

Producing a bar chart of total gifts per day

You can print a simple bar chart of total gifts per day as follows:

1 On the **Reports** tab click **New**.

2 Highlight the **Chart Wizard**, select **Gifts for .... Appeal** from the Choose Table or Query list and click **OK**.
You will be asked 'Which fields contain the data for your chart?'

3 Select **Amount** and **Date** and click **Next**.
The next question is 'What type of chart would you like?'

4 Select the top left picture, **Column Chart**, and click **Next**.

5 On the Preview Chart screen, double click the horizontal axis description **Date by Month**, change it to **Day** and click **OK**.

6 Click **Next**.

7 Leave the Chart Title defaulted and click **Finish**.

8 The chart appears and you will be able to print it, save it and give it a Report Name.

OTHER REPORTS

You can produce many and varied reports with a combination of the queries and reports functions in Access and you will have to decide what you really need. The above serves only to give you an idea of what is possible with very little time and effort.

EXPORTING A REPORT TO WORD OR EXCEL

It is possible to export data from tables, queries and reports for further manipulation in Excel. You may wish to incorporate your report (or a table or a query) into a Word document, perhaps for publishing in a newsletter. Alternatively, you may wish to analyse it further using Excel, for example to produce high level summaries related to Nominal Ledger account codes. Access provides direct links for these functions.

- On the Reports tab of the Database window, highlight your report and click the **Preview** button.

- On the tool bar immediately above the report there is an **Office Links** icon. If this icon is set to **Word** and you want to export the report to **Excel** (or vice versa), then click the **drop down arrow** beside the icon to change it.

- Clicking the **Word** or **Excel** icon exports your report immediately into a Word document or an Excel spreadsheet and transfers you to Word or Excel so that you can work on the document or spreadsheet straightaway.

- **Closing** the document or spreadsheet takes you back to the database.

Adding new contacts to the database

With this Access database, adding contacts can be done at any time by selecting the first menu item from the switchboard, clicking the ▶ ✳ button and entering the details of the new contact.

Chapter summary

You have now set up your Access database and completed a full cycle of recording contact details, mailing, recording income and analysing income. You can now go round the loop as many times as you like. Some of the actions described in this chapter will not be required on the second and subsequent cycles, for instance setting up the Queries, because you have them in place and they only have to be modified and/or re-run.

CHAPTER 8

A more advanced database in summary

This chapter is a summary of the detailed instructions given in the previous two chapters. Its purpose is to act as a guide for experienced Access users who do not need step by step instructions but merely need ideas on the way the system can be set up and used. You can refer back to the detailed chapters if you need to at any time because the sub-headings below are the main sub-headings of the relevant chapter.

Creating a more advanced fundraising database (Chapter 6)

We will be using Access to create a complete fundraising database to deal with the research, strategy, monitoring and analysis of your campaign. To do this we need to set up tables (data files), link the tables together so that they can be used together, create data entry forms and link the forms together so that we can find our way around the database easily. We will also use Word for mailing purposes and reports, and data can be transferred automatically into documents from Access.

SETTING UP AN ACCESS DATABASE AND CREATING YOUR TABLES

Open Access and choose the option to create a new Blank Database. From the Tables tab of the Database window, create five new tables: Contacts, Appeals, Gifts, Communication Log and Notes.

Linking the tables together

You will link the tables together using the Relationships function (Relationships icon or tools menu). Add all five tables to the Relationships window. Start by editing the relationship which already exists between Appeals and Gifts. Then create relationships between Contacts and Gifts, Contacts and Communication Log, Contacts and Notes (in all three cases the link field is

Contact Number). In all four relationships ensure that the following are set: Enforce Referential Integrity, Cascade Update Related Fields, Cascade Delete Related Fields and Join Type = 3.

SETTING UP ACCESS FORMS FOR ENTERING AND VIEWING DATA

Data can be entered to Access tables in a 'datasheet' mode, but entering data via forms is a more powerful method and is more attractive and flexible: you can combine fields from several tables on one form whereas a datasheet relates to one table only.

Create a series of forms for entering data. Start with a simple columnar form for all the fields in the Appeals table using the Forms Wizard. Similarly create a form for all the fields on the Contacts table.

Now create a single form for entering (and viewing) gifts, communications and notes together:

1 Start by using the **Forms Wizard** to create a Justified form with enough fields from the Contacts table to uniquely identify a Contact (for instance Contact Number, Title, First Name, Other Initials, Surname, Job Title, Organisation and Postcode). Extend the borders of the form as much as possible.

2 Use the **Tab Control** button to add two tabs to the form. Name the first tab 'Gifts and Communications'. Name the second tab 'Notes'.

3 On the **Notes** tab create a Subform with all the fields except Contact Number from the Notes table.

4 On the **Gifts and Communications** tab create two Subforms, one with all the fields from the Gifts table (except Contact Number) and the other with all the fields from the Communication Log table (except Contact Number).

MAKING IT EASIER TO NAVIGATE THE DATABASE

To finish off our database and make it easy to use we need to link the Contact-related forms together and create a menu (known as a switchboard in Access) that will come up when the database is opened.

How to link two forms together

The Contact-related forms are the Contacts form and the Gifts, Communications and Notes form. To link them:

1 From Design mode in the Forms tab, add a **Command Button** to the Contacts form.

2 Label this button **Page 2**, choose **Form Operations** from the Categories list and **Open Form** from the Actions list, then select the **Gifts**, **Communications and Notes** form. Clicking this button on the main Contacts form will immediately open the Gifts, Communications and Notes form.

3 Now put a command button on the Gifts, Communications and Notes form labelled **Close Form** (or Return) by using the Category, **Form Operations** and the Action, **Close Form**.

4 For convenience you could also put a **Find** button on the Contacts form – Category: **Record Navigation** and Action: **Find Record**.

Creating a switchboard

Create a switchboard from the Switchboard Manager item under Database Utilities in the Tools menu. Put an item for each of your forms on the switchboard plus an Exit Database item (Command – **Exit Application**). Put as the first item on the list the form you will use most, for instance the main Contacts form. Make your new switchboard the default and set your switchboard to be displayed every time you start the database by using the Startup item in the Tools menu.

RECORDING AND VIEWING INFORMATION ABOUT YOUR SUPPORTERS

Data can now be entered into any of the forms and the powerful Find function can be used on any field in any table. You could set up the very first Contact ie record number 1 to be the Anonymous Donor – enter Anonymous in Surname and leave all the other fields blank. It will be easy to find and add gifts to if it is Contact Number 1.

Using a more advanced fundraising database (Chapter 7)

Once the database has been set up and details of your Contacts have been recorded you need procedures to be able to use the information in an effective manner.

RECORDING COMMUNICATIONS WITH CONTACTS

Go into the database, select the first item on the Switchboard, find the Contact you wish to record something about by using the Find button, click the Page 2 button and enter the details on the appropriate subform.

MAILING

To mail a standard letter to everyone on your database, you create your letter in Word and use the Mail Merge function from the Tools menu. From Get Data in the Mail Merge Helper window you select Open Data Source, find your Access database and select Contacts on the Tables tab. Continue as normal with the Mail Merge function.

To mail a standard letter to a selected group or sub-set of Contacts, you proceed as above but before you merge, you use the Filter Records function within the Query options of the Mail Merge Helper to select the Contacts you require. You need to do this because every data field in the Contacts table is available to you.

RECORDING INCOME

If you have a small number of donations to enter then: go into the database, select the first item on the Switchboard, find the first Contact you wish to record a donation against by using the Find button, click the Page 2 button and enter the details on the Gifts subform.

If you have a large number of donations to enter then you may wish to use the Gifts form if you created one.

SENDING THANK YOU LETTERS

Before you can send thank you letters you have to select the Contacts from whom you received donations on the day in question. You use the Access Query function for this. The easiest way is to use the Simple Query Wizard to create a Query that selects all Gift records along with their appropriate name and address details from the Contacts table. Save the Query with a name like 'All Gifts', run the Query, then use this Query as the Data Source in a Word mail merge. You can then use the Filter Records function in Mail Merge to print letters for records with only the relevant day's gifts. (This will exclude anonymous gifts.)

Without using the Filter Records function at all, you can use the full Access Query function to create a Query that selects only today's Gift records (not the anonymous gifts) with the appropriate name and address details and then do a Word mail merge. Using the full Query function is much more complex than using the Simple Query Wizard, but it is a useful skill to learn because it will allow you to produce more complex selections of records from your database.

ANALYSING INCOME

Almost any report you can imagine can be produced with the Access Reports function but below are three simple ones to be created using the Reports Wizard.

Top donors report

To produce a report of the largest donations, use the All Gifts Query as the input to the Reports Wizard. Select the fields you want printed, select descending order on the Amount field, preview the report and print just the first page.

Gifts this month

To produce a summary report of gifts this month, copy the All Gifts Query and in Design mode enter a logical expression to represent this month in the Criteria cell under Date. Use this new Query as the input to the Reports Wizard. Select the fields you want printed, sort and summarise by date and select Print Summary Only.

Gifts this appeal

To produce a summary report of gifts for a specified Appeal, copy the All Gifts Query and in Design mode enter a logical expression to represent the appeal in the Criteria cell under Appeal Code. Use this new Query as the input to the Reports Wizard. Select the fields you want printed, sort and summarise by date and select Print Summary Only.

CHAPTER 9

Making more effective use of your database

By now you will have built your Access database. You will know how to use it and will probably have entered the details of several hundred contacts into it. This chapter gives you some hints and tips that will help you to use your database more effectively.

Improved navigation

You have a simple menu with four options on it (see page 94). However, with the first and third options (General Contact Information and Appeal Information) you have to click the tiny Close button to get back to the menu. Why not add a 'Return to Menu' button on each form? You do this by the following sequence: Forms, Contacts, Design, Command Button, drag and drop to create the button size and shape, Categories = Form Operations, Actions = Close Form, Next, click Text and overtype 'Close Form' with 'Return to Menu', Next, Finish. Repeat for the Appeals form.

Note that you might have to make the forms bigger (by dragging the edges) to create space for the new buttons. Also note that you do not have to do this for the second menu option (Gifts, Communications and Notes) because this already has a Close Form button on it. The effect of this button is that if you enter the form from the menu, then clicking the button will return you to the menu, whereas if you enter the form from the Page 2 button on the main Contacts form, then clicking the button will return you to the Contacts form.

Another improvement is to put a Find button on the Contact Gifts, Communications and Notes form. You do this by the following sequence: Forms, Contact Gifts Communications and Notes, Design, Command Button, drag and drop to create the button size and shape (Suggestion: put it near the top of the form, to the right of the Surname and Postcode), Categories = Record Navigation, Actions = Find Record, Next, Picture = Binoculars 2, Next, Finish. This button will be useful when you have a big batch of gifts to enter and you normally find records by searching for Surname or Postcode. **W**

Warning: If you add a Find button to this form, you will only be able to use it if you enter the form directly from the menu. If you enter the form from the Page 2 button on the main Contacts form, then it will not work!

Using the forms

During normal daily operations, when dealing with a small volume of data, say up to 20 cheques a day, it is always best to use the first menu option (General Contact Information) and then click the Page 2 button to enter details of gifts or communications or notes. This way, you can check everything you know about the contact (and make absolutely sure that it is the right contact) before you enter gift and other information.

When you have a large number of gifts to enter, then use option 2 of the menu (Gifts, Communications and Notes). If you add a Find button to the Gifts, Communications and Notes form, you can search for a contact by their Contact Number and get an immediate visual confirmation of their name and postcode by using this form for bulk data entry.

You may have noticed that the size of the columns on the Gifts subform and other subforms is not optimal. For example the Amount field will be wider than it really needs to be and you may have to scroll to the right to see all the gift fields. You can re-size the columns by dragging the right-hand edge of each column heading. Try it by picking up the right-hand edge of the Amount column and dragging it to the left to make the column narrower. Your changes are retained even when you close the database and open it again on another day.

The entries in the Gifts and other subforms are in the sequence you entered them to the database. Therefore they are most likely to be in date order, with the oldest first. This order can be reversed at any time by right-clicking anywhere in the Date column and clicking Sort Descending. This is useful if a particular contact is a long-time supporter of your organisation and has given a large number of gifts. You can also use this feature to sort the gifts from the supporter into value order by right-clicking anywhere in the Amount column and clicking Sort Descending. However, beware because these settings too are retained when the database is closed.

Default dates

You can eliminate the need to enter the date on every gift, communication and note record by getting the database to default to today's date. This is a good idea if, on most days, you enter these details on the day that they are received. If you need to enter a different date, then you can always overtype the date that the computer has inserted. One way to get the date to default to today's date is as follows: Tables, Gifts, Design, Date, General tab, type **Now()** into the Default Value box, Save, Close. Repeat for the dates in the Communication Log table and the Notes table.

Using the Find function

Warning: The standard Access Find function is extremely powerful. It is too powerful in some ways because it now includes a Replace function (similar to Word). This has the potential to do untold damage to your database. NEVER, NEVER USE THE REPLACE FUNCTION.

The Find box has three major parameters to help your search. These are: Find What, Look In and Match. (Ignore the More button.) **W**

- **Find What** is where you type the data you are looking for eg the Surname, the Contact Number, the Postcode, etc.
- **Look In** usually has two options. One is the name of the field that your cursor is pointing to and the second is the name of the form you are looking at. For the sake of simplicity, always ensure that this is set to the form name, which is 'Contacts' for the form associated with option one of the menu. This means that it will search for whatever you type into the Find What field in every field on the form for every record on the database. Don't worry about it, because for the number of records you have on your database, the difference in search time will be insignificant.
- **Match** has three options: Any part of field, Whole field and Start of field. Any part of field is most useful and in fact includes the other two. Start of field is particularly useful when looking for records where you have the first part of the postcode eg M3 or RG2.

The one problem with the standard Access Find function is the fact that you can only search for data in one field at a time. So don't search for things like 'smith'. Use the postcode instead.

Adding a Reports menu

Why not add a Reports menu so that every time you want to run a report you don't have to go behind the scenes to the Database window? You can do this as follows:

   1 Tools.

   2 Database Utilities.

   3 Switchboard Manager.

   4 New.

5 In Switchboard Page Name type 'Standard Reports' and click **OK**.

6 Highlight **Standard Reports** and click **Edit**.

7 **New**.

8 Type 'Top Donors Report' into Text.

9 In Command, select **Open Report**.

10 In Report, select **Top Donors**.

11 Repeat steps 7 to 10 for Gifts This Month report and for Gifts This Appeal report.

12 **New**.

13 Type 'Return to Main Menu' into Text.

14 Leave Command defaulted to **Go to Switchboard**.

15 In Switchboard, highlight the name you gave to your first switchboard (in our case it was **Appeal Contacts Database**) and click **OK**.

16 **Close**.

17 In Switchboard Pages, highlight the first switchboard you created (it will have **Default** in brackets beside it) and click **Edit**.

18 **New**.

19 Type 'Standard Reports' into Text.

20 Leave Command defaulted to **Go to Switchboard**.

21 In Switchboard, highlight **Standard Reports** and click **OK**.

22 In Items on this Switchboard, highlight **Standard Reports** (it will be at the bottom) and click **Move Up**. This will bring it above Exit Database on the menu.

23 **Close**.

24 **Close**.

The next time you come into your database, you will have a reports menu that you can access from your main menu and as you add new reports to your system you can add them to this menu.

Improving the reports

In order to make the **Gifts This Month** report more user-friendly you can get the system to ask you to enter the date range you want to report on instead of having to alter the Query every time. You can do this as follows:

1 Queries.

2 Gifts This Month.

3 Design.

4 Replace the expression in the Criteria box under Date with the following:
Between [Enter beginning date:] And [Enter ending date:]
(Note the use of square brackets).

5 Save.

6 Close.

7 Reports.

8 Gifts This Month.

9 Design.

10 Click the **Text Box** icon on the **Toolbox** tool bar (it looks like **ab**) and draw a box on the line next to the report heading by dragging.

11 Overtype Text99 with 'From' and type '[Enter first date:]' into the box containing the word Unbound.

12 Click the **Text Box** icon again and draw a box next to your beginning date by dragging.

13 Overtype Text99 with 'To' and type '[Enter last date:]' into the Unbound box.

14 Save.

15 Close.

The system will now prompt you for the first and last dates for your report. You will have to enter them twice; once for the query and once for the report heading but that is a small price to pay for the convenience of not having to modify the query every time you run the report.

In a very similar way you can alter the **Gifts for ...... Appeal** Query and Report to be generalised so that you enter the name of the Appeal when you run the report. You can do this by the following:

1 In order to avoid confusion in the future, change the name of both the Query and the Report to 'Appeal Summary' (you do this clicking twice, slowly – not double clicking, on the Query or Report name and then overtyping it).

2 **Queries**.

3 **Appeal Summary**.

4 **Design**.

5 Replace the expression in the Criteria box under Appeal Code with the following: [Enter Appeal Code:].

6 **Save**.

7 **Close**.

8 **Reports**.

9 **Appeal Summary**.

10 **Design**.

11 Click in the box containing the report heading and overtype it with 'Appeal Summary'.

12 Click the **Text Box** icon on the **Toolbox** tool bar and draw a box on the line next to the report heading by dragging.

13 Click in the Text99 box and hit the **Delete** key. This should remove the heading but still leave the box containing the word Unbound.

14 Click in the Unbound box and type '[Enter Appeal Code]'.

15 **Save**.

16 **Close**.

You can now get a summary of any appeal at any time directly from the menu.

Chapter summary

Your database will now be much easier to use on a day to day basis, as you will be able to carry out all operations from the menu. You will only need to go behind the scenes to the Database window if you want to create new queries or reports.

What next?

This section provides help and advice for two types of users of this book. Chapter 10 is aimed at those who have successfully created a database and are happily using it, but who are keen to extend their database and do more with it. Chapter 11, on where to go for help, is written for those who need additional help to create their database and includes advice for people who want to move beyond the scope of this book.

Extending your database

Once you have designed your first database you might get bitten by the bug and want to do more with Access, and perhaps explore other programming tools such as Visual Basic. (Alternatively, you might also say 'Never again!') Assuming that you do get on well with the databases outlined in this book, and you find them both useful and reasonably easy, then you might want to extend your database and the functions you perform with it. This chapter looks briefly at some of the extensions you could add.

Easy extensions to your database

GIFT AID

Now that every single gift from a tax-paying supporter qualifies for Gift Aid, you could add a few fields to your database to keep track of this potentially huge pot of additional income. A few simple extensions might be as follows:

- Add a Gift Aid Declaration flag (a Yes/No field) to your main Contact record with a default value of 'No'.
- Add a Declaration Date to the Contact record.
- Add a Withdrawal Date to the Contact record.
- Add a Tax Claimed (Yes/No) field to the Gift record (default to 'No').
- Add a Tax Amount Claimed (Currency) field to the Gift record.

You can then fill in these new fields as and when appropriate and modify your reports to include the tax figures. You can get far more complex than this by adding different declaration types, adding a Tax Table and making automatic tax claims, but you are now getting to the level at which you should be looking at a packaged fundraising system.

RECORDING INCOME BY FUNDS

The SORP (Statement of Recommended Practice) accounting requirements demand that you can record your income by different 'funds', particularly, restricted and unrestricted ones. Most people link specific Appeals to specific funds, that is one Appeal benefits one fund only, although there can be many Appeals for that fund. In this case, the Appeals table we defined and used earlier (see page 78) is all you need, but if one Appeal could benefit several funds then you might want to add another table to your database. This Funds table would be linked to Gifts in exactly the same way as the Appeals table is linked, and you would have to enter a Fund Code on every gift, exactly as you enter an Appeal Code (or choose from a list of values).

LINKING A CONTACT'S INTERESTS

When we created the Contacts table we added a data field called Contact Type. This is fine for a unique attribute of the contact eg Company or Individual. But what would be particularly useful is a table where you can see linked together the interests of a Contact, for instance you see immediately that someone is a regular donor AND helps out at events AND is interested in your work in Africa. You can do this by simply adding another table with a one to many link from the Contacts table, so that a contact can have many interest records associated with them. All you need in the table is a Primary key (let the system create this when you save the definition), the Contact Number and an interest indicator which you create as a pick list. You can then select people with particular interests/characteristics to contact.

LIFETIME VALUES AND OTHER SUPPORTER STATISTICS

You will soon (hopefully!) find that you have large numbers of supporters, each of whom has given you many donations over a period of time. It is useful to know how much they have given in total (lifetime value), how many times they have given, their average gift value, their highest gift value, their lowest gift value etc. These statistics can all be calculated and stored on the contact's main record. The lifetime value can even be calculated in our simple database where all the gifts are stored in an Excel spreadsheet. All you have to do is sum across every value column of the spreadsheet.

DIARY ACTIONS

In a similar way to creating the Interests table, you can create a Diary Actions table which you can use to record actions completed or future actions related to your contacts. (This could all go in the Communications Log table if you want to keep it simple.) You can then use this as a reminder list by finding all the actions for today, tomorrow, this week, next week etc.

EVENTS AND ATTENDEES

The idea here is to set up a table listing the events you hold and a table for guests who are invited/attend the events. The Events table is easy. You simply set it up in exactly the same way as you set up the Appeals table. The Attendees table is set up in exactly the same way as you set up the Gifts table. You create a one to many link from Events to Attendees and another one to many link from Contacts to Attendees. Some of the data fields you put into your Attendees table might be: contact number, event code, date invited, date accepted, number of tickets purchased, attended Y/N and notes/comments.

LEGACY DETAILS

The average legacy case is open for many months, and sometimes years. If you have a lot of legacies then you might want to create a simple table to record the legacy type, amount expected, executor, next of kin, date of will, date probate granted, date of next contact, etc. This table can be used to monitor and control the progress of the legacy, and even to provide a simple form of cash flow if you maintain details of the amounts you expect and when you expect them.

More complex extensions to your database

CONTACT RELATIONSHIPS

Many of your contacts will be related to each other in a variety of ways, for instance family relationships and business relationships. You can create a Relationships table that links contacts together. The table will consist of little more than contact number one, relationship one, contact number two and relationship two. For example: 123, Father/Son, 456, Son/Father. Both contact numbers are linked to the contact number in the Contacts table and both relationships are chosen from the same table which, for every relationship entered into it, contains a reciprocal relationship (in the above example this would be Father/Son and Son/Father).

NON-DUPLICATE ADDRESSES

For both Outlook and Access as defined earlier in this book, the address is contained in the contact's record. If you have two contacts at the same address, you create two records each containing the same address, ie the address is duplicated. What happens when you get a contact who has more than one address? Outlook allows for three addresses per contact and we could do the same in our Access database by having three addresses in our Contacts table. What we have here is a many to many link between contacts and addresses, in other words a contact can have many addresses and an address can have many contacts. This can be resolved by creating a separate Address table and creating a linking table (similar to the Attendees table above) that links an address with a contact. However, if you are going this far then you are either very experienced with Access or you should be thinking of a proper packaged system.

OTHER ACCESS TABS

You may have noticed there are three tabs on the Access Database window, Pages, Macros and Modules, that we haven't used yet. Pages refers to special types of Web pages for viewing and working with data. This is too advanced for us at this stage. If you feel confident, then try out Macros. A macro is a series of stored instructions that perform particular tasks. An example might be: open a table, sort the table in a particular order and run a report. The Modules tab allows you to integrate Access commands and Macros with the Microsoft Visual Basic programming language, as well as with other Microsoft Office 2000 programs. Leave this one to the experts!

CHAPTER 11

If you need help

Perhaps you have followed this book slavishly and you are still having problems. Or, maybe you have outgrown the simple nature of this book and want to know what to do next. Where do you turn? What do you do (that doesn't cost a fortune, of course)?

Where to find help

BOOKS, VIDEOS AND CD-ROMS

First, try your local bookshop. There are many books on Microsoft Office and even more on Access. Obviously, some are better than others, but buy a couple and see how you get on – £15 or £25 is a small price to pay for that vital clue which helps you make progress.

Tutorials for Office and Access are available on video and CD-ROM. If you cannot get these through your bookshop, look at some PC magazines where they are often advertised.

UNIVERSITIES, COLLEGES AND SCHOOLS

Second, sound out your local universities, colleges or schools with a sixth form. Most will have students studying computer science. Many of them are studying Access in particular. Beware, however, because they might be on an earlier version of Access and not be completely familiar with what you are doing. Anyway, it is certainly worth a try.

OTHER VOLUNTARY ORGANISATIONS

Third, talk to other voluntary organisations. The larger ones are likely to have specialist computer staff and the smaller ones are likely to have someone who has, through necessity, become more than just 'IT literate'. You will soon find someone familiar with Access who might be able to help you.

THE INTERNET

Fourth, the Internet. There are numerous web sites and discussion groups to check out that can give you free help. In particular, try the Microsoft web site at www.microsoft.com

TRAINING COURSES

Fifth, go on training courses. A full day of training can cost from as little as £70 per person per day. Many training companies run public courses on Microsoft Office and on Access. When considering these, make sure that every student/delegate gets a PC of their own for the day for maximum effectiveness. Some training companies will do a course just for you in your own office from £500 (not too expensive when you think that you can put five or six people on it). Talk to other voluntary organisations to find out which training companies they recommend.

THE PROFESSIONALS

And finally, as a last resort, try a software house or a consultant. These people will be professionals in the computing field, and although many specialise in narrow aspects of the business, if one can't help you another will be able to. But remember, they might be able to solve your problems but they will cost you several hundred pounds per day!

Packaged fundraising database systems

If you have been through this book and you find that:

- you really can't get on with it, or
- you have used it and exhausted its possibilities, or
- you want to go far beyond what is covered in it (and, quite frankly, we have only scratched the surface of what a full-blown fundraising system can do)

then, you should be considering a specialist packaged system.

Warning: There are some systems available for less than £1,000, but they tend to be rather limited in what they can do.

These cost from £4,000 upwards with the most popular ones costing £12,000 to £15,000 for a four-user system including implementation and training. **W** There are, in fact, more than 80 systems that can reasonably call themselves fundraising (or contact) databases, not just the two or three that are mentioned all the time. If you are thinking of this route then:

- shop around;
- see what other voluntary organisations are using;
- take your time;
- get advice;
- be absolutely clear about what you want before you see a salesperson;
- write down your needs (not wants);

- be prepared to compromise (no system is perfect);
- take up references;
- be prepared for a long period of upheaval and, most of all,
- be prepared to put in a very large investment of personal time and effort.

Where to find information on the Data Protection Act

You can contact the Information Commissioner at:

Office of the Information Commissioner
Wycliffe House
Water Lane
Wilmslow
Cheshire
SK9 5AF

or telephone: 01625 545700
or look up the website: www.dataprotection.gov.uk

Final word

If you have managed to read this far through the book then you are very dedicated and you probably have a pretty good database and are in a position to help others.

Good luck!

Glossary

Access	A database product from Microsoft Corporation aimed at the smaller organisation and/or smaller system.
CD-ROM	Compact Disk – Read Only Memory. Similar to a music CD but containing programs and data that a PC can read.
Database	A collection of related information.
Drop down list	A window showing a single item from a list plus a downward pointing arrow. Clicking the arrow opens up the full list and any item from the list can be selected. The selected item will then be displayed in the window.
Excel	The spreadsheet package supplied by Microsoft Corporation.
Export	The act of taking data out of your database in order to use it in another system eg in an Excel spreadsheet.
Field	An individual item of data which may be contained in a column of a database table eg town, county or postcode.
File	A related set of records eg a file of name and address records.
Folder	Synonymous with File. One of many introductions with Windows systems to make the computer more 'user-friendly'.
Gb (Gigabyte)	One billion characters of information.
Icon	A picture to represent a computer program or function instead of words.
Import	The act of bringing data into your database from another computerised source eg from an Excel spreadsheet.
Internet	A world-wide link-up of computer networks which allows the exchange of information in a common format.
K (Kb – Kilobyte)	One thousand characters of information.
LAN (Local Area Network)	A network of local computers, typically in the same building.
Mb (Megabyte)	One million characters of information.
Menu bar	A bar with words (rather than icons) usually starting with File and ending with Help, each of which when clicked with the mouse, open up to give more options.
Network	Two or more computers connected together so that they can exchange information.

Outlook	A multi-purpose package supplied by Microsoft Corporation that includes functions for diary, to do list, notes and contact management.
RAM **(Random Access Memory)**	Computer memory that you can read from and write to.
Record	A set of related data items or fields.
Relational Database	A collection of related information that is organised as a table or as a series of related tables.
ROM (Read Only Memory)	Computer memory that you can read but cannot alter.
Spreadsheet	A page of tables (columns and rows) of data, usually numeric, that can be manipulated by a spreadsheet program such as Excel.
Stand-alone	A term used for a computer which is not connected to any other computer.
Subfolder	A sub-set of records from a folder eg only the names and addresses of our corporate contacts.
Tape Streamer	A tape drive, similar in many ways to an audio cassette tape machine, that is used to 'back up' the information on your hard disk.
Visual Basic	A graphically-based programming language that can work in conjunction with Access.
Word	The word processing package supplied by Microsoft Corporation.
Worksheet	Synonymous with spreadsheet – a single page of rows and columns.

Other publications from DSC/CAF

DSC/CAF 'How to' guides

These titles are available from the Directory of Social Change, Publications department, 24 Stephenson Way, London NW1 2DP. Call 020 7209 5151 or e-mail info@dsc.org.uk for more details and for a free publications list, which can also be viewed at the DSC website: www.dsc.org.uk

Prices were correct at the time of going to press but may be subject to change.

ORGANISING SPECIAL EVENTS
for Fundraising and Campaigning

John F Gray & Stephen Elsden

Special events are an enjoyable way for voluntary organisations to raise money and public awareness. But what makes an event successful? The authors draw on their extensive experience to lead you through the process of:

- setting objectives and finding an innovative idea
- planning and budgeting
- choosing venues and recruiting patrons
- dealing with the public and talking to the media

Illustrated by case studies from the British Red Cross and other major charities, this is an invaluable guide for major event organisers and committee members.

1st edition, 2000
£10.95, ISBN 1 900360 56 X

LOOKING AFTER YOUR DONORS

Karen Gilchrist

When someone makes a donation to your good cause, that should not be the end of the story – but the beginning of a long relationship. This book is about building those relationships. If you look after your donors, the chances are that you will raise more money from them in future. Using real-life case studies, this guide shows you how to:

- plan your programme of donor development
- analyse your supporter base and research other potential donors
- secure repeat donations and new support
- evaluate how well you look after your donors

Whether you are a single fundraiser or a member of a specialist department, you will find plenty of practical advice on building relationships with organisations and individual donors.

1st edition, 2000
£10.95, ISBN 1 900360 76 4

FIND THE FUNDS
A New Approach to Fundraising Research

Christopher Carnie

This book answers the key question that all fundraisers ask: 'Where is the money?' It guides you through the research process, showing you the best places to look for inside information about trusts, individuals and companies. The book includes:

- a sources list with details of more than 120 publications, web-sites and agencies which can help
- an appendix of photocopiable charts for planning research and recording data

The author demonstrates how a focus on finding the funds takes the fear out of fundraising. With practical advice on time and resource management, and on using the information once you have got it, this book will enhance the professionalism of any fundraiser.

1st edition, 2000
£12.95, ISBN 1 900360 54 3

FUNDRAISING FROM GRANT-MAKING TRUSTS AND FOUNDATIONS

Karen Gilchrist & Margo Horsley

Grant-making trusts and foundations are set up to give money to charitable activities. The challenge for any fundraiser is to put an effective case for support by showing how their particular project matches the aims of the trust. This book takes you through:

- the origins and work of grant-making trusts

- putting together a project proposal and researching appropriate trusts
- the application and assessment processes
- working with trusts that have agreed to fund you

The emphasis throughout is on providing step-by-step advice and examples of good practice. Details of helpful organisations, publications and sources of advice are also included. An appendix highlights the major trusts in the UK, with a brief summary of their main grant areas.

1st edition, 2000
£10.95, ISBN 1 900360 77 2

Index

NOTES

NOTES